# The ICSA
# Charity Trustee's Guide

**Jane Arnott**

Published by ICSA Publishing Ltd
16 Park Crescent
London
W1B 1AH

Typeset in Sabon & ITC Franklin Gothic by
Paul Barrett Book Production, Cambridge

Printed and bound in Great Britain by
TJ International Ltd, Padstow, Cornwall

British Library Cataloguing in Publication Data

A catalogue record for this book is available from the British Library.

ISBN 1-86072-193-1

*To Austin, for keeping the house clean and me happy.*

*To Mum and Dad, for teaching me the value of the 'voluntary principle'.*

# Contents

# How to use this book

## Who this book is for

The aim of this guide is to support trustees of small to medium-sized charities within their role. It covers the key aspects of the trustee function that are common to the majority of trustees. As such it will also be of interest to charity managers and organisations' professional advisers. Whilst focussing on charities, much of the information will be relevant to the not-for-profit sector as a whole.

## What it will cover

Every organisation, like every person, is individual but there are areas of commonality. Some of these are determined by law, others by good practice. This guide will cover those issues that will potentially impact on all charities at some point in their existence. Areas covered by the guide include the recruitment of trustees, trustees' responsibilities, issues of good practice in trusteeship, the functioning of the board, financial issues (including fundraising) and the evaluation of a charity's work.

Organisations can be complicated and inevitably a publication of this nature will not be able to answer every question that may be raised by a trustee of a not-for-profit charity. However we hope to give you a better understanding of the wider issues and to point you in the right direction when it comes to determining the detail of your charity.

## Charity reform

A major review of charity law was conducted by the Cabinet Office's Strategy Unit in 2002, leading to wide-ranging proposals for legislative change, contained in the Strategy Unit's report *Private Action, Public Benefit*. Implementation of those proposals that are adopted will take place over a number of years. The potential changes are explained in boxes throughout the guide and trustees are advised to keep track of developments through the voluntary sector press and websites.

## Finding your way around

The different chapters of this guide provide the background to the issues addressed as well as some practical tools that you can use in your organisation. Tips, model and sample documents, notes of caution, checklists and examples are given in the boxes in each chapter. The examples given are based on real case studies of voluntary organisations but have been adapted for the sake of illustration and confidentiality.

At the end of the book there is a Directory containing a list of further information sources.

## Disclaimer

This book is aimed at trustees of small and medium charities. Although every effort has been made to ensure the accuracy of the information contained in the book, it is a general guide and does not attempt to give specific advice; rather, it is intended to give an overview of the issues facing trustees. Trustees should not rely solely on the information provided in this book in the course of their decision making. As is stated at various points in the guide, trustees should undertake further research and seek professional advice as necessary. No liability will be accepted for any loss or damage caused as a result of organisations or individuals acting on information contained in this publication.

# 1 Starting point

## INTRODUCTION

This chapter lays the foundations for the rest of the book. We will look at the definition of charity and of trustees, the different terms used in the not-for-profit sector and their meanings. We will also consider the range of legal structures available for voluntary organisations and the legal framework for charities, including some of the wider legislation that impacts on the sector.

## What is a charity?

The huge variety of charities means that a 'charity' is one of those concepts that is difficult to define – but you know one when you see it. Charities differ greatly, but there are some fundamental principles that are common to all and these can help us in describing a 'charity'.

### Public benefit

Charities must operate for the public benefit. The public benefit brought about by the charity may relate to the public as a whole or to a sufficient section of the community. For example, a Citizens' Advice Bureau offers services that are accessible to the public as a whole, whereas an organisation providing services to people with a specific disability is supporting enough of the community to be considered to be operating for the public benefit. This holds true even if the number of beneficiaries is very small, for example, a medical charity relating to an extremely rare disease.

Whilst a degree of private benefit is acceptable, this should be incidental to the central purpose of the charity and should not undermine the benefit to the public. For example the payment of salaries to charity staff for the work they do in order to achieve the charitable objects is an acceptable private benefit. In contrast, organisations which exist to distribute profit or benefits amongst their membership cannot be charitable, as the benefit is not available to the public as a whole or to a sufficient section of the community. Consequently, profit distributing companies cannot be charitable, although they may undertake some charitable activities. In addition, certain clubs that exist to provide services or benefits to their members (e.g. exclusive sport clubs) are also excluded.

The expectation that charities should operate for the public benefit is supported by the 'voluntary principle' of trusteeship, requiring that those responsible for governing charities should not benefit from the charity. This 'voluntary principle' determines that those with the responsibility for the charity hold that charity's assets and the organisation as a whole 'on trust' (hence the title 'trustees') and must therefore act in the best interests of the charity. In order to act in the charity's best interests, trustees must avoid any conflicts between their personal interests and those of the charity. The problems caused by conflicts of interest and suggestions of how such conflicts can be managed are discussed in chapter 2.

## Charities' independence

Conflicts of interest are not limited to the personal circumstances of trustees. Charitable bodies should act in the best interests of their beneficiaries and to do this they must, as far as is possible, be independent of external influence. Obviously charities operate within a wider social and economic context and it can be difficult in some situations to find a balance between the needs of beneficiaries in the short term versus the longer term and the needs of the organisation itself. It is for trustees to find this balance whilst avoiding external influence or control from other bodies, such as statutory agencies or commercial bodies. For example, although a charity funded by a local authority to provide services to the community may have to account to that authority for the quality and volume of the service provided under the funding, the charity itself should not be controlled by the local authority. Similarly a grant-making charity that is established by a company in order to distribute a proportion of its profits may operate to a broad grant-making framework or set of priorities that was determined by the company as part of the charity's inauguration but it should not be controlled by the company. Within its

---

**CASE EXAMPLE**

An independent charity was founded by a company and receives a percentage of that company's profits as its sole source of income. The charity makes grants according to the objects identified in its governing document. The charity's objects clause identifies its principal areas of interest, which include advancing education, training, medical research and the provision of social welfare services in local communities. The objects clause makes no reference to the wishes of the sponsoring company in terms of the distribution of funds.

---

constitution, the trustees of the charity must determine the detail, exercising their independent control in deciding which applicants should receive a grant. Any more intrusive control on the part of the originating company would fetter the discretion of the trustees and undermine the independence of the charity.

See chapter 4 for more information on governing documents.

### Political activities

Charities may undertake some political activities but must not be founded on political objectives. This principle is based on the premise that charities must operate for the public benefit and it is not for the courts (the ultimate arbiters of charitable status) to determine whether a political purpose will benefit the public; rather, such arguments are the stuff of political debate and Parliamentary decision. Consequently, political bodies that exist to change law or policy are generally considered not to be charitable. However charities can undertake limited political activities and this is discussed in more detail in chapter 2.

## The heads of charity

Not every organisation that appears to have philanthropic purposes can register as a charity. Charitable purposes were first defined by an act of Parliament in 1601 but the four 'heads' of charity used today were identified by a legal ruling in the *Pemsel* case in 1891 (*Commissioners for Special Purposes of the Income Tax v Pemsel* [1891] AC 531). These have, of course, since been refined and elaborated by case law and

Charity Commission decisions but the four key headings remain the same:

1 the relief of poverty;
2 the advancement of education;
3 the advancement of religion; and
4 other purposes beneficial to the community.

For the first three heads (relief of poverty, advancement of education and advancement of religion) there is a presumption that the public will benefit, either directly or indirectly, although this presumption can be challenged in individual cases. Organisations seeking to fall under the fourth head will need to establish that their purposes will provide public benefit.

## Relief of poverty

The relief of poverty has been widely interpreted over the years and is not restricted to absolute financial poverty, but may include relative financial poverty (e.g. charities for 'distressed gentlefolk') and those suffering hardship or distress. Consequently charities for people with disabilities, refugees and other socially excluded groups often fall under this heading.

## Advancement of education

Organisations which exist to promote education may be considered charitable. The education in question does not have to be formal education and can include other means of training, development and research. For research to be considered charitable it must be conducted in an objective and impartial manner and the public must have access to any useful results arising from the research.

Organisations falling under this heading are presumed to offer public benefit as educating individuals is generally considered to be beneficial to the public as a whole. Even if access to the education itself is restricted, e.g. to those paying a fee, the organisation may still be considered charitable on this basis. The case for charitable status may be further supported by making elements of the organisation's facilities available to the public as a whole (e.g. sports fields) or offering education to those from disadvantaged communities through scholarships and similar initiatives. Such is the reasoning behind the charitable status of private schools.

Educational or quasi-educational activities which cannot be seen objectively as offering public benefit will not be considered charitable, so propagandist and political activities do not enjoy charitable status, nor do clubs promoting hobbies that cannot be demonstrated to have educational value.

## Advancement of religion

The promotion of religion is considered charitable on the basis that belief in and worship of a deity, together with spiritual well-being, is beneficial to the public as a whole. Activities of charities falling under this head include the running and staffing of places of worship.

Within this heading, distinctions are not made between different faiths, with major world religions such as Islam, Judaism and Christianity being included. However the requirement that the religion must be founded on belief in a supreme being or beings and involve worship as an expression of that belief has resulted in the exclusion of some groups. In addition, the presumption of public benefit may be rebutted where the activities of the organisation are entirely private (as in the example below) or where the religious beliefs in question contradict the common principles of religion or morality.

A number of organisations providing specific services, such as education, social care and overseas aid, are founded on religious principles and rooted within a particular faith but also fall under the other heads of charity because of the nature of their work.

**CASE EXAMPLE**

The Church of Scientology was refused charitable status by the Charity Commission on the basis that, although Scientologists believe in a supreme being, their activities did not constitute worship and were not beneficial to the public. The Church's practices of audit and training were considered to be more akin to counselling and study than veneration or reverence of a deity and as such did not represent worship. The limited access to the Church's activities and the private nature of the beneficial effects of the audit and training practices meant that the Church's application failed on both the advancement of religion head and the requirement for public benefit.

## Other purposes beneficial to the community

This 'catch-all' head has been interpreted widely to reflect changing times. Areas such as racial harmony, urban regeneration and recreation have been included, whilst bodies such as gun clubs have lost their former charitable status. Organisations falling within this category have to demonstrate public benefit, as there is no underlying presumption.

Organisations can fall under several different heads of charity or may be charitable if they meet just one of the criteria, as in the examples below.

| Organisation | Head of charity |
| --- | --- |
| A day care centre for older people who are disadvantaged by mobility problems, poor health and low income provides a daytime meal, access to health and social care on site and a range of activities, including religious celebrations and training in IT skills. | Relief of poverty; advancement of religion; advancement of education. |
| An arts centre stages concerts, theatre performances and exhibitions. | Advancement of education. |
| An informal peer support group for people with mental ill health. | Relief of poverty (this head includes illness and other forms of disadvantage, not just financial poverty). |

---

**PROPOSED CHANGES – CHARITABLE PURPOSES AND PUBLIC BENEFIT**

The Cabinet Office Strategy Unit's review of charity law has resulted in proposals to redefine charity. The four heads of charity would be replaced by ten new purposes:

1 the prevention and relief of poverty;
2 the advancement of education;
3 the advancement of religion;
4 the advancement of health;
5 social and community advancement;
6 the advancement of culture, arts and heritage;
7 the advancement of amateur sport;
8 the promotion of human rights, conflict resolution and reconciliation;
9 the advancement of environmental protection and improvement; and
10 other purposes beneficial to the community.

In addition, all charities would be subject to a public benefit test and this would be checked on an on-going basis.

These changes would require new legislation.

## Not-for-profit organisations that are not charities

There are many not-for-profit organisations that are not charities. This may be because they confer some type of private benefit, as is the case with social enterprises and credit unions. Although these organisations may not have the strict profit-making motives of commercial bodies, the fact that the purpose of the organisation includes a significant element of personal gain excludes them from charitable status.

Many other not-for-profit organisations are not registered charities or subject to Charity Commission controls because they fall within the remit of other regulators. This will be discussed in more detail later in the chapter when we consider charity law, but Registered Social Landlords (often in the form of housing associations) are a common example of such an organisation. Although these organisations form an active part of the charity arena on local and national levels, they are often not registered as charities because they are constituted under separate legislation.

## What is a trustee?

Historically, one of the significant problems of charity trusteeship was that many trustees were unaware of their legal responsibilities. The difficulty was often one of nomenclature as there are many different titles used for the trustee board, such as management committee, council of management, executive committee, board of directors or board of trustees. Essentially, those with the ultimate responsibility for and control of the organisation are the trustees as they administer the organisation 'on trust' for the beneficiaries. This body should be defined in the governing document.

It is the trustees' function to govern the charity and collectively they form the governing body. They are responsible for determining the direction of the charity within the framework laid down by the governing document. Elements of this function include ensuring financial viability and the achievement of the charity's aims. The responsibility of trustees will be considered in more detail in chapter 2, but equivalents would be e.g. the non-executive director of a commercial company or a local authority councillor.

## Legal framework

### Legal structures

When looking at the legal basis of a charitable organisation, a common mistake is to confuse an organisation's legal structure with its charitable status. Organisation structure and charitable status are separate elements. Just because an organisation is unincorporated does not make it charitable. Just because an organisation is a company does not make it commercial in nature. Charitable status looks at the issues discussed at the beginning of this chapter – for example, is the organisation operating for the public benefit, does it fall within the four heads of charity, and so on? Charitable status is determined by the outward looking objects of the organisation and, in the case of registered charities, is confirmed by registration with the Charity Commission.

The legal structure of the organisation is concerned with its internal structure and functioning, particularly in relation to the governing body, and is determined by its governing document. Often, an organisation's legal status will be confirmed by registration with another regulator, e.g. limited companies will be registered at Companies House.

The table on pp. 9–11 below gives further information on the different legal structures available to charities.

### Legal personality and limited liability

A charity may select any one of a number of available legal structures. The most appropriate structure for a particular charity will depend on a number of factors, the most common being the activities of the charity and the potential liability of its governing body. The key features that a charity should consider when selecting its legal structure are legal personality and limited liability.

*Legal personality.* All individuals over the age of 18 have legal personality. This means that they can enter into contracts, sue and be sued. Not all organisations have legal personality. Where there is no legal personality, as in the case of unincorporated associations, it is the trustees as individuals who have to act on behalf of the organisation, for example by being party to contracts. In contrast, in incorporated bodies such as limited companies, it is the organisation that enjoys legal personality and can enter directly into contracts.

*Limited liability.* Legal personality determines the liability of trustees. Where the organisation has no legal personality and trustees must enter contracts on behalf of the organisation, the liability of the organisation, which is essentially the trustees, is unlimited. This leaves the trustees personally open to legal action, for example in the event of breach of contract or an act of negligence. In the case of organisations that do have legal personality it is the organisation itself, rather than the trustees, that can enter into contracts and be sued. Liability is limited to the assets of the organisation and the trustees are not personally liable unless they have acted wrongly or negligently.

The table below gives an overview of the principal legal structures available to not-for-profit organisations.

| Legal structure | Governing document | Characteristics of the structure | Liability of trustees | Common examples |
|---|---|---|---|---|
| Trust | Trust deed | Trusts are normally established to administer funds or property, e.g. following a bequest. The trustee board tends to be small in number and appointed rather than elected. | Unlimited | Grant-making bodies; organisations that manage a particular property, e.g. a community centre or playground. |
| Unincorporated association | Constitution or rules | A body of trustees appointed (and often elected) by a wider membership who are sympathetic to the objectives of the organisation. | Unlimited | Community organisations, traditional providers of welfare services, user groups and sports clubs. The majority of charities have this legal structure. |

| Legal structure | Governing document | Characteristics of the structure | Liability of trustees | Common examples |
|---|---|---|---|---|
| Company limited by guarantee | Memorandum and articles of association | A board of directors elected by the membership. Members must subscribe to the memorandum and articles of association and their details are maintained in a register of members. Members guarantee to pay a nominal sum (usually around £1) towards the settlement of debts in the event of company insolvency. Guarantee companies are subject to the terms of the Companies Acts 1985 and 1989 and are regulated by Companies House. | Liability is limited to the assets of the company and the guarantees of the members. | Larger organisations, especially those with extensive contractual relationships (e.g. for staffing, service provision or premises) or operating in high risk arenas. This form of structure has become more popular as charities have taken on local authority contracts for services and trustees have grown more aware of their potential liabilities. |
| Incorporation by Royal Charter | Royal Charter | This form of incorporation is only, in effect, available to well-established organisations of national significance. | Limited | Professional institutes, e.g. ICSA and old established charities such as SSAFA |

| Legal structure | Governing document | Characteristics of the structure | Liability of trustees | Common examples |
|---|---|---|---|---|
| | | Royal Charters are the responsibility of the Privy Council. | | Forces Help. Organisations that have attained Royal Charters in recent years include the Prince's Trust and the Chartered Institute of Personnel and Development (CIPD). |
| Incorporation by Act of Parliament | Act of Parliament | Limited to quangos and similar organisations. | Limited | Universities, museums and organisations established for public purposes, such as distributors of lottery funds to good causes. |
| Industrial and Provident Societies | Rules | Organisations must have a community purpose, but often some form of member benefit is allowed, e.g. co-operatives. | Limited | Housing associations, co-operatives, friendly societies such as building societies. |

**CAUTION!**

Whatever the legal structure of the charity, the trustees' liability will not be limited if they act outside the law.

Any of the legal structures described above may be used by charitable organisations, but none of them were designed specifically for that purpose. Social, political and economic changes in the last century have radically altered the nature of the nation's not-for-profit sector. Some charities are now multi-million pound bodies with responsibility for the delivery of mainstream public services, but none of the legal structures available are an ideal fit. Trustees, understandably keen to limit their personal liability, often select to incorporate as companies limited by guarantee, but this exposes registered charities to double (and inconsistent) regulation from the Charity Commission and Companies House. Proposals for new forms of incorporation for not-for-profit organisations are discussed in the box below.

**PROPOSED CHANGES – LEGAL STRUCTURES**

The Strategy Unit has recommended the introduction of the Charitable Incorporated Organisation (CIO). The CIO would be a limited liability structure designed specifically for and available only to charities. The structure would be available in foundation and membership formats so that it could be used by charities with or without a membership and provisions would be introduced to ease the transfer from existing legal structures into the CIO. The CIO structure would not be available to charities in Scotland or Northern Ireland.

In recognition that the law governing Industrial and Provident Societies is outdated, the Unit has recommended revisions that will keep IPS legislation up to date with relevant aspects of company law whilst offering greater protection for organisations' assets. IPSs would be renamed under one of two categories: Community Benefit Societies or bona fide co-operatives. This would reflect the emphasis on either community or mutual benefit.

The Unit has also recommended a new legal structure for community based, not-for-profit social enterprises: the Community Interest Company.

All of these recommendations require legislative change.

Trustees considering moving their charity to incorporated status should check the development of the plans for CIOs and Community Benefit Societies before selecting their preferred structure.

## Governing documents and breach of trust

The table above lists the range of governing documents that may be adopted by charities and the potential liabilities to trustees. Trustees are advised to pay careful attention to the governing document of their charity. It is the foundation on which the charity rests and it sets the framework within which the charity operates, including the determination of the trustees' powers. Trustees operating outside the governing document and the powers vested in them may be acting 'ultra vires' (outside their powers) and/or in breach of trust. Depending on the exact circumstances of these actions, trustees may find that they are wholly and personally liable for any losses arising to the charity as a result.

For more information on preparing and using governing documents, see chapter 4.

## Charity law

Charity law is not consistent across the different countries in the United Kingdom. The box below lists the different jurisdictions and the legislation that applies.

---

### JURISDICTIONS WITHIN THE UK

Charities in England and Wales are principally governed by the Charities Acts of 1992 and 1993, supplemented by other legislation. They are subject to regulation by the Charity Commission. This book focusses on this legal and regulatory framework.

Scottish charities are subject to the Law Reform (Miscellaneous Provisions) (Scotland) Act 1990 and are regulated under the authority of the Inland Revenue. The regulation of charities in Scotland has been subject to review, so Scottish charities are advised to monitor any developments closely.

Charities in Northern Ireland are subject to the Charities Act (Northern Ireland) 1964 and the Charities (Northern Ireland) Order 1987. Their regulator is the Department for Social Development.

*Note that the legal requirements for Scottish and Irish charities are not considered in this guide.*

---

## Requirement to register

The Charity Commission is the body established by statute to monitor charities operating in England and Wales and to ensure that charities are operating in accordance with the requirements of charity law. Organisations are required to register with the Charity Commission if:

i    they have entirely charitable purposes *and have either*

ii   an annual income of more than £1,000; or

iii  own or occupy any land or buildings where such occupation is rateable (even if the local authority waives the rates); or

iv  have a permanent endowment (i.e. money, land or buildings given to organisations with a specification that the original gift shall not be spent);

*and*

v    are established in England and Wales; and/or

vi  the majority of trustees live in England and Wales; and/or

vii the majority of charity assets are in England and Wales; and/or

viii are incorporated in England and Wales (for companies only).

Charitable bodies established in England and Wales with income and property below this threshold are excepted from registration.

### Excepted and exempt charities

Excepted charities are those that do not have to register with the Commission. Charities are excepted from registration if their annual income does not exceed £1,000, they have no permanent endowment and do not own or occupy land. Registered places of worship are also excepted from registration.

Excepted charities may register voluntarily with the Charity Commission.

Exempt charities cannot register with the Charity Commission, even on a voluntary basis. They are exempt from the Commission's super-vision as they are usually subject to regulation by another body; however they continue to be bound by the general legal rules that apply to charities and certain statutory requirements. Exempt charities are listed in a Schedule to the 1993 Charities Act and include industrial and provident societies, universities and named museums and galleries.

---

**PROPOSED CHANGES – REGISTRATION THRESHOLDS, EXCEPTED AND EXEMPT CHARITIES**

The Strategy Unit has recommended that the threshold for compulsory registration should be raised from £1,000 to £10,000 and the criteria relating to permanent endowment and use of land should be scrapped. A charity below the registration threshold would be classed as a 'small charity' and would not be entitled to register.

Excepted charities above the registration threshold would be required to register.

The recommendations above require legislative change.

Under the proposals, the reports and accounts of exempt charities would set out how they hold and use voluntary funds, and the same level of information on exempt charities as is required of registered charities would be accessible via the Charity Commission website.

---

## Role of the Charity Commission

The Charity Commission is in the unenviable position of being both the friend and the regulator of charities in England and Wales. The essence of its role is to give the public confidence in the probity of charities. It seeks to do this by registering charities and supporting them through the provision of advice and information, monitoring charities through annual reporting arrangements and investigating those charities that appear to have acted improperly. The Commission maintains the Register of Charities and members of the public can view information on the Register. The easiest way to do this is via the Commission's website (www.charity-commission.gov.uk).

Where the Commission discovers cases of abuse or negligence it can intervene in a number of ways. For example, it may step in to administer the charity until the situation can be rectified or the organisation closed down. Currently the only means to mount an appeal against legal decisions of the Charity Commission is through the High Court.

Happily, most charities will never encounter the investigatory element of the Commission's role. For the majority of charities, contact with the Commission will be limited to annual reporting arrangements, occasional calls to the helpline and reference to the Commission's advice booklets.

## PROPOSED CHANGES – THE CHARITY COMMISSION

The Strategy Unit has proposed wide-ranging changes to the Charity Commission. Many of these seek to make the Commission a more transparent and responsive body. The recommendations include:

- the Commission to become a statutory corporation called the Charity Regulatory Authority;
- strategic objectives to be set out in statute;
- a statutory definition of the Authority's advisory role giving a clearer focus on regulation;
- the development of indicators to allow its performance against objectives to be judged and annually reported;
- open Annual General Meetings;
- board meetings to be open to the public;
- the inclusion of standard information about the largest charities on the Authority's website;
- the establishment of an independent tribunal to hear appeals against the Authority's legal decisions.

Many of these proposals require new legislation.

## Overview of charity law requirements

Charity law has evolved through statute and precedent over the past 400 years. We have already considered the crucial aspects of the four heads of charity and the need for charities to act for the benefit of the public. Other issues, such as reporting requirements, charity finance and fundraising will be considered in more detail in the later chapters of this book.

### Company law

Charities that are incorporated as companies limited by guarantee are subject to company law in addition to charity law. Key requirements include regulations regarding the running of general meetings, maintenance of registers and reporting to Companies House. Some aspects of the requirements for limited companies will be covered in the relevant chapters of this guide, but readers are also advised to refer to the ICSA Best Practice Guide *Guide to Guarantee Companies* and Malcolm Leatherdale *How to Run Your Charity* (ICSA Publishing Ltd, 1998).

## Other legislation

All not-for-profit organisations need to be aware of the range of legislation that may be relevant to their work. For organisations established under other statutes, such as Industrial and Provident Societies, the relevant legislation will apply, in this case the Friendly Societies Act. Charitable organisations will also be subject to any legislation that affects the work of their organisation. For example, organisations working with children and families will need to be familiar with the provisions of the Children Act 1989 and other family law legislation, while those providing day care, domiciliary services or running residential and nursing homes will operate under the National Health Service and Community Care Act 1990.

All organisations will be subject to general laws relating to issues such as health and safety, equal opportunities and employment, and these will be discussed further in the following chapters.

# 2    Responsibilities, regulation and risk

## INTRODUCTION

As trustees have overall authority for their charity, their responsibilities are wide ranging. In this chapter, we will consider these responsibilities, and the trustees' role in governing the charity and complying with relevant legislation and regulation. We will also deal with some of the minefields that confront charities, such as conflicts of interest and political activities.

## Responsibilities

### TRUSTEES' DUTY OF CARE

Trustees are generally required to act in the best interests of the charity. If trustees have any special knowledge or experience or act as trustees in the course of their job or profession, they are required by statute to use reasonable skill and care in relation to their background experience in certain situations. These situations are limited to financial management issues such as:

- investment (see chapter 8);
- acquiring land (see chapter 8);
- appointing agents, nominees and custodians (see chapter 8);
- insurance; and
- auditing (see chapter 7).

It is, of course, good practice for trustees to make good use of all of their skills, knowledge and experience in all areas of the charity's work.

### Governance

It is the role of the trustees to govern the charity. This leadership role is complex and wide ranging, so the following examples are illustrative, rather than exhaustive. It involves:

- keeping the charity true to its objects and to the governing document;

- ensuring the organisation's probity;
- being accountable for the charity;
- planning for the future of the organisation; and
- monitoring activities and outcomes against objectives.

The practical interpretation of this function will vary from one charity to another and, within a charity, is likely to shift over time. In some organisations, particularly smaller groups with few or no paid staff, trustees may be heavily involved in the daily administration of the organisation; in others they may work purely on the 'high level' basis of directing policy and ensuring the charity's efficacy. However it is interpreted, the trustees' governance role makes them responsible for the organisation. They are the ultimate decision makers with the final responsibility for directing the charity.

## Accountability

As a charity's ultimate governing body with legal responsibility for the organisation, the trustees are accountable for the charity as a whole. This accountability is universal. Whether the charity is being questioned in law, or by the public, donors, beneficiaries or any other party, it is the trustees who will eventually be held to account, as they are the final decision makers. Many charities underline the trustees' governance and accountability functions by appointing trustees through direct election, voted by the constituency of charity members.

## Policy/strategy

One of the governance functions of trustees is to determine the route that the organisation should take in seeking to achieve its constitutional objects. Obviously the direction and approach taken by a charity will change over time, subject to both internal and external influences. It is the function of the trustees to monitor such influences and decide on the best approach for the future of the organisation and the needs of its beneficiaries. Commonly trustees achieve this through developing plans, such as business plans, for implementation by staff and volunteers.

Business planning is a huge subject in itself and cannot be comprehensively covered in a book of this nature. However, it is a critical element of the trustee's role and the box below gives an overview of the process and content of typical business plans.

## BUSINESS PLANNING

### Why?

Used in the corporate sector as a means of convincing banks to invest in a company, business plans have now become common currency in the voluntary sector, for largely the same reason – many funders require them. Yet properly planned and implemented, business plans are a valuable means by which voluntary organisations may determine and achieve their goals.

Voluntary organisations exist in a constantly shifting environment and the voluntary sector often prides itself on its flexibility and its swift response to change and social need. In this context it can be easy for charities to drift off course, perhaps to meet a newly emerging need or to chase a readily accessible source of funds. However, it can also be easy for charities to take the course of least resistance, for example by continuing to deliver the same services by the same method for many years. Business planning provides a framework within which organisations can thoroughly review themselves, their activities, and the influences of the external environment. On the basis of such a review and taking their constitutional purpose as a foundation, charities can determine their future direction, both in terms of their ultimate objects and how these are to be achieved.

### What?

The business plan should serve a dual purpose as a planning and working document for the organisation itself and as a means of convincing potential funders to support the charity. As such, it needs to cover the following areas.

1 *The starting point* – i.e. an analysis of the charity as it currently stands, including its constitutional purpose, its track record and a thorough evaluation of its activities and services.

2 *The external environment* – this could include changing social needs, competition from other organisations, new opportunities and any other factors that will influence the future of the charity.

3 *The strategy* that the charity is adopting. What is the ultimate goal and how does the charity intend to get there? The business plan should consider the overall aims of the organisation and, within those aims, any smaller objectives. The plan should explain the relationship between the different objectives and identify priorities. The strategy may also define areas of work that the charity does not intend to undertake.

4 *Resources* – the business plan should also consider how the

*cont.*

## BUSINESS PLANNING continued

charity intends to resource its future, including staffing implications, premises and financial projections. The financial aspect of the business plan should include budgeted expenditure and income predictions, and many plans include cash flow forecasts. Financial planning is discussed in detail in chapter 7.

5 *Implementation and monitoring –* business plans should be working documents and the plan itself should contain information as to how the plan will be implemented. Risks that may prevent the charity from delivering the plan's objectives should also be discussed and the plan should also explain how implementation will be monitored. Many charities plan on a three to five year basis, although a longer period may be appropriate for organisations undertaking large-scale capital projects. Plans should be reviewed on a regular basis to take account of progress and changing circumstances. Monitoring and evaluation criteria and systems for the services and activities delivered under the business plan should be established at the outset and included in the plan. Monitoring and evaluation are discussed in detail in chapter 10.

6 *Capacity –* charities should demonstrate, for their own benefit and that of funders, that they have the capacity to deliver the business plan's objectives. This may include details of the skills and experience of the trustees and key staff, as well as any plans for further increasing organisational capacity.

### How?

The process of business planning can be as valuable as the end product itself. It is important to establish a baseline for the plan and as a starting point the organisation should consider its purpose. Agreeing a mission statement can be a useful way of reaching a shared understanding of the purpose of the organisation and communicating this to all stakeholders. In order to review existing activities and to consider the impact of external factors, it will be necessary to collect a range of information. This may include internal monitoring and evaluation reports, external studies and user surveys. Organisations should also undertake an analysis of their strengths and weaknesses, the opportunities available to them and any threats facing the organisation (known as a SWOT analysis).

From the base of the agreed mission statement and the analysis

*cont.*

21

## BUSINESS PLANNING continued

of internal and external pressures and trends, the charity can build its strategy. Once the trustees have decided what the charity is to achieve and how, they can then consider if it has the capacity to achieve its objectives and how these will be resourced. This is likely to be an iterative process and different elements of the plan may need to be revised and revisited in order to achieve a realistic, cohesive plan.

### Who?

In order for business plans to function as working documents it is important that those affected by them should have a sense of ownership of, and commitment to, the end result. It is therefore important for the planning process to involve stakeholders as well as the governing body. As a minimum, the trustees should be involved in discussions regarding the mission statement, strategy, priorities and resource implications and must have ultimate approval in these areas. They should also actively monitor the implementation of the plan.

In organisations with professional staff, the staff will normally manage the planning process and all charities should seek the input of staff and volunteers. This is essential in relation to those elements of the plan that impact on their work. It may also be advisable to seek the views of users and other stakeholders, perhaps through a formal consultation exercise.

## CASE EXAMPLE

A council for voluntary service had taken on a number of activities at the request of the local authority. All the activities involved the provision of services to individuals in the community and as such were not directly related to the organisation's key role of supporting the local voluntary sector. The board of trustees became concerned that the work involved in delivering direct services was detracting from the charity's core function and so included in its business plan the express provision that the organisation would not take on any more activities of this nature.

Running parallel to the business plan should be policies and procedures appropriate to the charity's work. These may be items that stand in their own right, separate from the business plan, e.g. disciplinary and grievance procedures for staff, confidentiality policies, and so on, or they may be an integral part of the plan and the objectives it seeks to achieve. For example, an organisation seeking to increase the number of service users from black and minority ethnic groups should include an equal opportunities policy as part of its business plan. It is the function of trustees to be involved in the development of policies, to approve the agreed policies and to monitor their implementation.

Monitoring and evaluation criteria should be integral to the development of business plans. This is also true of any policies, procedures and internal changes to the organisation. Implementation of internal changes, the impact of services, and the impact of any changes to services, should be assessed against the original aims. It is the responsibility of trustees to set the criteria against which activities will be evaluated, to identify the data necessary for evaluation to take place and to ensure that systems are established to collect and record the necessary data. Monitoring and evaluation are covered in more detail in chapter 10.

In staffed organisations, employees often play a key role in developing plans and policies. It is entirely appropriate that those involved in service delivery should have an input into organisational development, as they will have a more practical understanding of client need and the methodology of service delivery than many trustees; however, it remains the responsibility of trustees to steer the organisation in the right direction. Whilst staff input should be welcomed, information and suggestions presented by staff should be carefully examined and thoroughly debated within the wider context of the trustees' vision and ideas. The final decisions must be actively made by the trustees, not directed by staff. Chapter 6 looks in more detail at the boundaries between the roles of the trustees and staff.

## Finance

Trustees are responsible for the financial health of the organisation. Although the detailed requirements of bookkeeping and accounting may be delegated to a member of staff or an appropriate professional, it is the trustees who bear ultimate responsibility for ensuring that charitable funds are spent on charitable purposes. Trustees' responsibilities also include the more prosaic requirements of financial reporting, budgeting and securing sufficient income to run the organisation.

Another element of this financial responsibility is to maximise the income available from assets and investments held by the charity. This will include decision making regarding, for example, investments, trading activities and the use of property.

Financial management and reporting, fundraising and other financial issues are considered in detail in chapters 7 to 9.

## Employment

If the organisation employs staff, the trustees are employers. In the case of an unincorporated association, this responsibility rests directly with the individual trustees. In charitable companies, the company is the employer. Obviously there are many legal issues relating to the employment of staff, but in charities the situation can be further complicated due to the often blurred distinction between the trustee and staff roles and the fact that trustees cannot fully delegate their responsibilities to employees.

Staffing issues will be discussed in more detail in chapter 6.

## Marketing and public relations (PR)

Charities depend on their reputations. A good reputation is crucial to fundraising, the recruitment of staff and volunteers, and gaining the trust of the beneficiaries. Although hard to measure in financial terms, for many charities their reputation is their greatest asset. Consequently, it is critical that trustees oversee the charity's PR strategy. It is the trustees who should determine both the purpose of the organisation's marketing and PR strategy and the image of the charity and the charity's clients that any advertising or publicity campaign seeks to convey. Is the strategy designed to:

- increase the charity's income,
- raise awareness of an issue,
- raise awareness of the organisation, or
- establish 'market' dominance for the charity, i.e. ensure that the charity is selected over its competitors when people donate funds or volunteer?

It is particularly important for trustees to adjudicate the debate between operational and marketing demands. It is tempting to tug at public heart strings by portraying beneficiaries as victims. However, many beneficiaries will resent being presented in this way and those responsible for delivering the service may feel that such an approach unduly simplifies often complex issues and undermines the achievements of many beneficiaries. It is the trustees who are responsible for ensuring that the image communicated is mutually beneficial for the organisation and the users of its services.

---

**CASE EXAMPLE**   Marketing vs operational objectives

A large charity working with a wide range of beneficiaries ran several projects providing services for young people leaving social services care ('care leavers'). The marketing and PR department of the charity saw great opportunities for media coverage (and potential fundraising rewards) in human interest stories about care leavers. Without consulting the project workers, the marketing and PR department launched a campaign that portrayed the care leavers in simplistic terms. It implied that all care leavers were completely cut off from their families, unable to care for themselves adequately and unsupported by statutory agencies.

The reality was somewhat different and care leavers started to phone the projects to complain. Many of the care leavers still had contact with their families but these relationships were fragile and the media coverage had only served to increase tensions. Statutory agencies who were actively working with (and often funding) the projects in order to improve services for care leavers also objected.

The campaign had failed to improve understanding of the complex issues affecting care leavers and subsequently involved operational staff in extensive work to rebuild relationships with clients and partner agencies.

The trustees had approved the campaign following presentations from the PR director. They had not sought the opinion of operational staff and so had failed in their obligation to act in the best interests of the organisation as a whole.

---

Trustees are also responsible for ensuring that the cost of any marketing or public relations campaign can be justified against the planned benefits. Trustees should always be alert to cost:benefit considerations, but this is particularly important in relation to marketing and PR where costs can be very high, and benefits nebulous. For this reason, the measurable benefits which it is hoped will accrue from any campaign should be clearly defined at the outset.

As a charity depends on its reputation, any damage to that reputation can present a very real risk to the charity. Damage to the reputation of the charity, whether based on reality, rumour or perception, can be very hard to repair. Trustees need to be alert to the risk of damage and manage it appropriately. It may be worth developing a contingency plan to deal with the effect of such damage, if it should occur. This may include building up a list of named media contacts and ensuring that the charity has ready access to PR professionals. Such a plan will be particularly valuable if the charity has a high profile, works in a politically sensitive field, or undertakes inherently risky activities, such as outdoor education, medical care and disaster relief.

**tip**

One of the ways to reduce the risk of damage to your charity's reputation is to take the 'tabloid test'. This involves analysing your organisation's activities and considering them through the eyes of the tabloid press. For example, how would a tabloid paper report a decision to make a grant to a repeat offender? Asking this question does not have to stop you from making the grant, or undertaking any other potentially controversial activity, but it may help you to plan how to counteract any adverse publicity that may follow.

### Risk management

Risk management is a crucial element of trustees' work, although many board members would not call it by this name. Experienced trustees will be familiar with the need to balance the opportunities available against the risk, cost or potential negative impact of those opportunities. Although many risks have a financial implication, they are often presented in terms of threats to other aspects of the organisation and its function, such as its reputation, operation, achievement and personal safety. The following sections on regulatory issues and risk have a bearing on trustees' responsibilities in terms of risk management. Financial risk management is discussed in chapter 7.

Trustees must assess the level of risk and decide on the appropriate action to take in order to prevent damaging eventualities occurring and to mitigate the effect if they do. To do this, the trustee should begin by looking at the organisation from a variety of angles, which will help to identify the full range of risks faced by the charity. It is useful to go beyond the board of trustees to draw on the experience of staff and volunteers who are involved with the everyday activities of the organisation. They will be able to identify operational risks. Third parties, such as funders and users, may be able to help identify some of the external and environmental risks. It can be helpful to manage this process by dividing the risks into different categories, for example:

- governance, e.g. conflicts of interest for trustees;
- operational, e.g. staff shortages;
- financial, e.g. poor cashflow;
- environmental or external, e.g. damage to a charity's reputation;
- compliance with law and regulation.

When dealing with risk, trustees need to achieve a proper balance. Paranoia about risk can paralyse an organisation whilst a laissez-faire attitude can lead to detrimental, and even tragic, outcomes. Once risks have been identified, look at two factors in respect of each risk:

- the probability that the risk will occur; and
- the impact of the risk, should it happen.

The following table may be a helpful tool in achieving the right balance between paralysis and laissez-faire and identifying those risks that require active management and those that can be accepted. By grading both the probability and the impact of a risk as high, medium or low, risks can be placed in priority order. Allocating a numerical value to the grades helps to further define priorities, so scores of 1, 2 and 3 are awarded for low, medium and high probability or impact. Multiplying the two scores creates a 'risk total' with the highest scoring risk becoming the top priority.

| Likelihood of risk occurring | Impact of risk, should it occur | Score |
|---|---|---|
| High – 3 | High – 3 | 9 |
| Medium – 2 | High – 3 | 6 |
| Low – 1 | High – 3 | 3 |
| High – 3 | Medium – 2 | 6 |
| Medium – 2 | Medium – 2 | 4 |
| Low –1 | Medium – 2 | 2 |
| High – 3 | Low – 1 | 3 |
| Medium – 2 | Low – 1 | 2 |
| Low – 1 | Low – 1 | 1 |

The nature of the risk, its probability and its potential impact will determine how trustees should respond to it. High scoring risks are likely to need countermeasures as a means of managing the risk. This could be:

- *prevention* of the risk happening, for example by stopping the risky activity;
- *reduction* of the probability or impact of the risk, e.g. by increasing security or implementing risk reducing procedures; or
- *transferring* the risk elsewhere. The classic example of transferred risk is insurance, which transfers the financial impact of a risk from the insured to the insurer.

Trustees may decide to accept low scoring risks. Although these risks should not be ignored completely, they are unlikely to require much active management. Trustees may also decide that some of the preventative or risk reduction measures required to combat higher scoring risks are unacceptable, and so accept the reduced measure of protection. For example, placing bars on windows reduces the risk of break-ins but can create an unwelcoming atmosphere and may impede fire safety. In deciding not to install window bars, a reduced level of protection against burglaries is accepted.

As has been mentioned in relation to risk of damage to the charity's reputation, it may be necessary to develop a contingency plan to deal with the effect of an identified risk should it arise. This approach is particularly suitable for risks that would have a high impact.

## CASE EXAMPLE

An organisation working with distressed and confused clients who are dependent upon medication faces a high possibility that, without appropriate procedures, clients may be given or take incorrect medication. This could have a high impact in terms of the beneficiaries' health so the risk should be managed, ideally by the introduction of procedures for administering and recording clients' medication and managing any emergencies that arise. Such procedures have the added advantage of protecting staff and volunteers from the accusations of confused clients and should be supported by appropriate personnel arrangements.

In this case, the trustees might reduce the risk by the development of a medicines procedure and institute a contingency plan in the form of an emergencies procedure.

As well as dealing with individual risks, risk management processes can inform the strategic approach of the organisation as a whole. By identifying and categorising all the risks facing the charity, a clear picture of the balance of risk within the organisation can be developed – this is known as a 'risk profile'. A risk profile showing a large volume of high risk activities may indicate that certain areas of the charity's work or function should be reviewed. Similarly a proliferation of low risk activities may imply that the organisation is being unduly conservative. The process may also help trustees to determine their 'risk tolerance', i.e. the level of risk that they are prepared to accept. This will vary between and within charities. For example, a charity with a stable funding base may be prepared to take a high financial risk in developing a new service, but be very cautious in protecting its reputation.

Risk management should be subject to regular monitoring to ensure that any changing risks are properly managed and that countermeasures are in place and continue to be appropriate. This process is best supported by a risk register. The register records the risk, its probability, its potential impact and the controls that are in place to manage it. The register should also record the name of the person responsible for managing the risk and the frequency of the risk management review, e.g. monthly, quarterly or annually.

## Regulatory issues

### Insurance

Appropriate insurances are a key part of financial risk management and in some areas are compulsory. Look at the full range of your organisation's activities and identify areas of risk when deciding which insurances are optional but necessary and which are legally required. For example, charities employing staff are legally required to have employers' liability insurance and should display the insurance certificate. Those working with volunteers and beneficiaries should have public liability insurance. Where the charity provides transport or requires staff and volunteers to use their own cars on charity business, trustees need to be sure that at least third party cover is taken in respect of each driver and that this cover is valid for charity business. Some insurance companies include within their standard policies cover for the use of the insured's car for volunteering or work but others require an additional premium for this type of cover.

Organisations occupying premises obviously need the necessary insurances, such as buildings and contents insurance. Where an organisation owns and occupies property, the organisation will be responsible for all insurances relating to the property. Where property is let to or from another party, insurance requirements are usually specified by the terms of the lease agreement. For example the landlord may be responsible for the fabric of the building, with tenants arranging insurance for their own possessions kept on the property.

Those running advice services should take out professional indemnity insurance to protect them against claims for losses arising from poor advice.

The activities of the charity will determine which further insurances should be secured. As with all insurance policies, it is important to inform insurers of the full range of charitable activity in order to ensure that all necessary policies are in place.

Trustees may also seek to protect themselves against actions arising out of their trusteeship through trustee indemnity insurance. As with all policies, trustees should consider the level of risk against the cover offered by the insurance in order to justify the cost. Trustee indemnity insurance is a trustee benefit and as such must be allowed by the governing document.

Trustees need not arrange insurance cover themselves, this task may be delegated to staff, but trustees should ensure that appropriate cover has been secured and is maintained, for example by viewing insurance certificates. Copies of insurance documentation should be kept off site.

The following checklist summarises the areas trustees should consider in relation to insurance.

---

## CHECKLIST

☑ What policies are required by law?     e.g. employer's liability, third party vehicle cover

☑ What policies are required under the charity's contracts?     e.g. buildings insurance

| | | |
|---|---|---|
| ☑ | What policies are needed in relation to the charity's activities (both permanent and ad hoc)? | e.g. professional indemnity, public liability |
| ☑ | What policies are needed in relation to the charity's assets? | e.g. buildings insurance, contents insurance |
| ☑ | What other policies might be needed? | e.g. trustee indemnity insurance |
| ☑ | Who has responsibility for arranging insurance? | Ensure that this is documented and clearly communicated to the individual concerned |
| ☑ | Are all policies current? | Check all certificates at regular intervals |
| ☑ | Do all policies represent good value for money? | e.g. is the cover worth the premium, or could you get better value with a different insurer? |
| ☑ | Where are policy documents kept? | This should be clearly recorded and should be off site |

## Health and safety

Trustees are responsible for health and safety within the organisation. This includes the health and safety of any staff, volunteers and those using the service. If the charity employs staff, the health and safety law poster (available from the Health and Safety Executive) should be displayed. A health and safety policy may also be required.

The need to develop a health and safety policy is not exclusive to organisations undertaking high risk activities, such as providing adventure holidays for young people or working with people with challenging behaviour. Nor is it restricted to the occupation of premises: for example, groups undertaking outreach, home visiting or detached work need to pay particular attention to personal safety of volunteers and staff due to the fluid, unpredictable and unstructured nature of client interaction. In fact, all organisations should have a written health and safety policy and this is a legal requirement for those with five or more employees. The policy should consider the activities undertaken by the organisation, the working environment and the nature of the client group.

All employers (and self-employed people) are required to assess risks from work activities. Where there are five or more employees, any significant findings of the risk assessment must be recorded, so the health and safety policy should discuss those risks and identify means of minimising risk and addressing problems as they arise. Regular health and safety audits, preferably by an external body, are also advisable to ensure that the policy is being followed and that the working environment is safe.

The sorts of issues that should be covered by a health and safety policy are discussed below. However this is not a comprehensive list. Some organisations will need to consider a wider range of issues and many of the points covered will not be relevant to some charities.

Trustees are advised to physically protect their staff, volunteers, and beneficiaries, and to financially protect themselves by developing and implementing an appropriate health and safety policy and ensuring that those affected by it receive relevant information and training.

Appropriate arrangements should be made to deal with any accidents or emergencies that do occur at work. This includes first aid provision in the form of suitably trained individuals and necessary equipment. Such provision should be used to cope with minor injuries and to manage more serious cases until medical help arrives.

All accidents and emergencies should be recorded and many organisations keep an accident book for this purpose. By law you are required to report certain injuries and diseases to the Health and Safety Executive or the environmental health department of your local authority. These include death, major injury (including certain fractures and dislocations), 'over three day' injuries (i.e. the employee cannot do his or her normal job for three or more days as a result of the injury) and certain work-related diseases. Dangerous occurrences that could have led to a reportable injury must also be reported.

Work-related stress can be a serious problem in voluntary organisations and trustees who employ staff have a legal obligation to address this issue, for example by reviewing workloads and giving employees sufficient autonomy regarding the planning of their work and time.

Trustees are advised to seek specialist advice on health and safety issues. The Health and Safety Executive has an extensive range of free information to help you meet your obligations in relation to health and safety (see the Directory for details).

| Area of work | Issues to consider |
| --- | --- |
| Premises | Alarms and evacuation procedures, including use of fire extinguishers, access to fire exits and emergency assembly points; corridors and stairs to be unobstructed; tripping and slipping hazards, such as trailing cables, loose carpets, wet floors etc.; adequate lighting; adequate heating/cooling systems and ventilation; safe noise levels; safe electrical equipment, gas appliances, kitchen equipment etc.; manual handling, e.g. lifting or moving equipment or furniture; security of the building and personal safety issues such as policies on lone working and office hours |
| Work stations and VDU use | Lighting that ensures adequate illumination whilst minimising glare; ensure set up of desk, chair and computer minimises risk of back strain or repetitive strain injury; ensure adequate breaks from VDU use and make vouchers available for sight tests and prescriptions |
| Working away from the office | Travel arrangements that maximise personal safety (e.g. use of own vehicle versus public transport or travelling in pairs); office based records covering issues such as destination, expected time of return and emergency contact numbers; mobile phones and attack alarms; identity cards for staff; arrangements for working in the evening/overnight |
| Working with the public | Guidance on lone working; training on identifying and dealing with risk situations; selecting whether to visit a client in their own home or an alternative venue; ensuring that staff maintain clear escape routes; advice on manual handling (for example if providing personal care to clients) |
| Outings, centre-based and residential activities | Ratio of staff and volunteers to clients; vetting and criminal record checks on staff and volunteers; appropriate training for staff and volunteers; parental consent for activities involving people under 18 years old; risk assessment; policies regarding substance misuse (e.g. refusing admission to people under the influence of alcohol or non-prescription drugs); policies regarding administration of medication and self-medication; information regarding any medical conditions; emergency procedures; emergency contact numbers |

## Data protection

The Data Protection Act 1998 controls the way in which organisations manage any information held that relates to individuals. The legislation covers computerised data and any manual records held as part of a 'relevant filing system'. Not-for-profit organisations that retain information on individuals, whether they be staff, volunteers, trustees, beneficiaries, members or donors, are subject to the legislation and trustees are responsible for ensuring that the law is complied with. The principles central to the legislation include the following:

- Data must be processed fairly and lawfully: this means that there must be a legitimate basis for processing the data and that the processing must be fair. The 'fair processing code' considers the ways in which data is obtained. This includes the requirement that the identity of the data controller (i.e. the organisation holding the information) and the purposes for which the data is being processed should be available to the data subject, together with any other information necessary to ensure fairness. Many charities manage this requirement by providing an explanation of the ways in which any data will be used and offering individuals an opportunity to opt out of these uses by ticking a box. Data may be processed without consent in order to protect the vital interests of the data subject, i.e. life or death situations.
- Data should be accurate and, where necessary, kept up to date. Where information is obtained from a third party, reasonable steps must be taken to ensure the accuracy of the data.
- Personal data should be processed in accordance with the rights of individuals. This means that individuals can request access to information about themselves and can request the prevention of data processing that is likely to cause damage or distress or will be used for direct marketing. Organisations can charge £10 to individuals for access to information held on them and must respond within 40 days of the request. Telephone and fax 'preference services' have been established so that people can register their objection to receiving unsolicited calls and faxes.
- Those holding data are expected to take appropriate security measures to ensure that data is not unlawfully processed, lost or damaged. This extends to relationships with third parties who

process information on another's behalf. Here, the security of data should be integral to the contractual relationship between the two parties.

- Data can not be transferred outside of the European Economic Area unless the destination country or territory ensures an adequate level of protection. Sensitive personal data requires further protection. This principle will be relevant to international not-for-profit organisations.

Organisations are required to notify the Information Commissioner that they hold personal information. Notification is subject to an annual charge and applications for notification must be made on a form that is available from the Commissioner's office. Exemptions from notification are available for the maintenance of a public register and for processing data for organisational administration, e.g. staff records. Trustees should consider whether notification is required in respect of their organisation. Even those organisations exempt from notification must still comply with the principles listed above.

The nature of trustees' responsibility for their organisations' activities and administration means that it is in their interests to ensure compliance with data protection requirements. The Information Commissioner issues enforcement notices in the event of non-compliance and may prosecute organisations that breach such notices. Individuals may claim compensation if damage or distress has been caused or if organisations are unable to prove that adequate care has been taken in processing data.

The following checklist highlights the key points that voluntary organisations should consider. Further information is available on the Information Commissioner's website at www.dataprotection.gov.uk.

## CHECKLIST

- ☑ Is there a legitimate reason for processing the data?
- ☑ Are your organisation's identity as the data controller and the purposes for which the data is being processed available to the data subject?
- ☑ Are data subjects able to opt out?
- ☑ If you process data without the subject's consent, is this necessary to protect the vital interests of the data subject?

☑  Is data accurate and up to date? How can you be confident of this?

☑  How do you ensure the accuracy of data obtained from a third party?

☑  What security measures are in place to protect data? Are these included in any contracts with those who process data on your behalf?

☑  Is notification with the Information Commissioner necessary or is the organisation exempt?

## Conflicts of interest

The founding principle of trusteeship is that trustees must act in the best interest of the organisation and not benefit from their trusteeship. As such, trustees are required to avoid any conflicts between their own interests and those of the charity. Conflicts of interest may take many different forms, as illustrated by the table opposite.

Conflicts of interest damage the ability of the board to make decisions that are in the best interest of the charity and can undermine board cohesion if board members feel that one of their number is seeking to influence decisions to his or her own advantage. Even where trustees have acted appropriately, if there appears to have been a conflict of interest, the reputation of the charity can be severely damaged. Consequently it is important for charities to identify potential conflicts of interest and prevent or manage any that arise. A register of trustees' external interests may be kept and regularly updated and trustees may be asked to sign a commitment to declare any interests that arise in the course of a charity's business. When such interests do arise, trustees should withdraw, not only from the decision making but also from the discussion, in order to ensure that they are not in a position to influence the final outcome. In addition, the organisation should not send the affected trustee any sensitive information in relation to the item in conflict. In these circumstances, even if the remaining trustees do make a decision to the advantage of the interested trustee, they can at least establish that the decision has been made properly and the conflict has been properly managed.

Situations may well arise where a decision which is in the interest of a trustee is also the best decision for the charity. In seeking to manage the conflict appropriately, charities should consider the 'tabloid test'

| Type of conflict | Description | Examples |
|---|---|---|
| Direct financial interest | A trustee's financial interest in an issue related to the charity is the most easily recognisable form of conflicting interest as it runs directly counter to the principle that trustees must not benefit from the trust. Here trustees will be benefiting directly from their trusteeship and this financial benefit is likely to affect objective trustee decision making. | – The payment of salary or professional fees to a trustee by the charity.<br>– The award of a contract to a company of which a trustee is a director.<br>– The sale of property to a trustee at below market value. |
| Indirect financial interest | This occurs when a close relative of a trustee's benefits from the charity. Here trustees will benefit indirectly if their financial affairs are bound with those of the relative in question through the legal concept of 'joint purse', as would be the case if the relative were the spouse, partner or dependent child of the trustee. | – Awarding an employment contract to a trustee's spouse.<br>– Making a grant to a trustee's dependent child. |
| Non-financial or personal conflicts | Here trustees receive no financial benefit but continue to be influenced by external factors. Conflicts of loyalty fall within this category. | – Trustees influencing board decisions on service provision to their own advantage, perhaps because they use the charity's service themselves or care for someone who does.<br>– Awarding contracts to friends of a trustee.<br>– Making a decision in favour of another organisation of which a trustee is a member, trustee or in some other way involved. |

discussed earlier in this chapter, i.e. 'How would this situation appear if reported in a tabloid newspaper?'

## Remuneration

The duty of trustees to act in the charity's best interest is intertwined with the 'voluntary principle' of trusteeship, i.e. that trustees should not be paid. The payment of trustees would present a conflict between the charity's interests and those of the trustees.

However, the level of responsibility carried by trustees, the amount of work involved in trusteeship and the difficulty of recruiting sufficient numbers and quality of trustees led to a Charity Commission review on whether the voluntary principle should be maintained. The majority verdict and the conclusion of the review was that the voluntary principle should be preserved, although there is limited provision for the payment of trustees, specifically for trustees' professional skills. The most frequently quoted examples are trustees who have legal or financial skills undertaking specific pieces of paid work for the charity (as opposed to being paid for being trustees), such as negotiating contracts. Other professionals are also included within the provision, for example, a trustee who is a builder may be paid for repairs to the charity's premises. Such payments must be specifically provided for in the charity's governing document (for more information see chapter 4). In all cases, the conflict of interest must be managed when deciding to make payments to professional trustees.

---

**PROPOSED CHANGES – TRUSTEE REMUNERATION**

In its review of charity law, the Cabinet Office Strategy Unit recommended that there should be a statutory power for boards to pay individual trustees for services outside their trusteeship, if the board believes such a payment to be in the best interests of the charity.

---

## Ultra vires/breach of trust

The trustee role is defined by charity law and the individual organisation's governing document. Acting appropriately within their legally defined roles provides trustees with an element of protection from legal action against them. Once trustees step outside the legal boundaries they may be acting ultra vires (i.e. outside their powers) or in breach of trust. In such circumstances the level of protection available diminishes and trustees become much more vulnerable to legal action. One of the defences available is to have acted in breach of trust but 'honest mistake', rather than negligence or wilful breach. However, trustees are advised to be familiar with the scope and limitations of their governing document and to act within it.

## Political activities

We said in the last chapter that political purposes are not charitable, although not-for-profit organisations can undertake political activities. In this section we will look at the limitations on political activities that apply to charities. Non-charitable not-for-profit organisations are not subject to restrictions on political activities.

Political activities are those actions which seek to achieve or oppose a change in law or government policy and decision. Any political activities undertaken by charities must conform to the following fundamental principles:

- the issue must be related to the charity's purposes or to the voluntary sector as a whole;
- there must be a reasonable expectation that the activity will help to achieve the charity's purposes or benefit the voluntary sector;
- the trustees must have the appropriate powers within their governing document to undertake the activities (see chapter 4 for more information about trustees' powers);
- political activities must be an ancillary element of the charity's work;
- resources expended on political work must be justified;
- political activities must be focussed on well-founded, reasoned argument based on experience or research;
- any research must be objective, conducted according to accepted standards of research methodology and published to educate and inform; and
- information and argument should not be merely emotive or designed to exert public pressure and must not be known to be inaccurate or have been distorted to illustrate a point in the charity's favour.

Charities must act independently of political parties and the government and they may not undertake any activities which support or oppose a particular party or politician or the government. Where a charity's opinion is in sympathy or opposition to a particular party, the charity should assert the independence of its opinion. The table below lists acceptable and unacceptable political activities for charities.

Any powers to undertake political activities will be vested in the trustees by the governing document and it is the trustees who are

## POLITICAL ACTIVITY

Subject to the basic principles discussed above, the following are acceptable political activities to be undertaken by charities:

✓ commenting on public issues
✓ dialogue with government
✓ publication of views expressed to government
✓ providing information to the public in support of a campaign
✓ providing information on the way in which MPs or parties have voted
✓ providing supporters with information and material to send to MPs and others
✓ conducting petitions
✓ responding to possible changes in law or government policy, including support or opposition for the passage of a Bill
✓ supplying MPs and members of the House of Lords with information for use in debate
✓ affiliating to campaigning alliances, provided the alliance undertakes only those activities that the charity could undertake itself

✓ employing Parliamentary staff and lobbying agencies
✓ commenting during elections
✓ seeking MPs' support for grants
✓ promoting or participating in lawful demonstrations and direct action which is limited to the promotion of reasoned argument and education (e.g. through speeches and leaflet distribution)

The following activities are not acceptable:

✗ seeking to influence public opinion in support or opposition of a political party
✗ organising or participating in party political demonstrations
✗ claiming evidence of public support on a political issue without adequate justification
✗ seeking to influence electoral voting
✗ participating in demonstrations and direct action outside the promotion of reasoned argument and education (e.g. marches)

**CASE EXAMPLE**

Many charities in the disability field campaigned for improved rights for disabled people during the debate on the Disability Discrimination Act 1995. Carers charities undertook similar activities during the discussion on the Carers Act. In both cases charities acted within the acceptable limitations as they were involved in political activities in pursuit of their objects, i.e. to improve the quality of life of their client group. In both cases alliances were formed.

responsible for ensuring that campaigns are within the terms of the governing document and the wider legal framework. Activities outside of these limitations could represent a misuse of charitable funds for which the trustees could be liable. This could involve the trustees being personally required to reimburse these funds together with any tax relief gained against them. The reputation of a charity and public support for that charity may also be damaged by improper political activities.

**PROPOSED CHANGES – GUIDANCE ON CAMPAIGNING**

The Strategy Unit has recommended that the Charity Commission guidance on campaigning should be less cautious and give greater emphasis to the activities that charities can legitimately undertake.

## Wrongful trading

Trustees often select the legal structure of a company limited by guarantee for their charity because it limits their personal liability. However incorporation offers no protection in cases of wrongful trading. This arises when an organisation continues to operate and enter financial arrangements even though it has inadequate assets to meet its liabilities (i.e. it is technically insolvent); for example if a charity enters into a contract to lease office space but cannot afford to continue operating or to pay the rent. Trustees' liability is not limited in these circumstances, so trustees must be fully aware of the organisation's financial health at all times.

Insurance is available to underwrite trustees' liabilities in the event of wrongful trading. As with all insurance policies, trustees should consider the risk against the cost and level of cover offered by the policy.

# 3 Recruitment, appointment and induction of trustees

---

## INTRODUCTION

Given the function of trustees, it is important to make sure that the initial stages of any trusteeship lay a solid foundation for the task ahead, ensuring that trustees fully understand their role and responsibilities, relating both to the concept of trusteeship and their specific work within the charity. This can be achieved through an effective recruitment, appointment and induction process which has the added advantage of helping new trustees to adapt quickly to their new role, enabling them to play a full part in the governance of the charity at an early stage. Such a process is clearly a governance, rather than a management, issue and as such should be led by the board itself.

This chapter looks at the recruitment, appointment and induction process. Issues such as the composition and diversity of the board, periods of trusteeship and the turnover of board membership are discussed in chapter 4.

---

## Recruitment

The combination of high workloads, significant responsibilities and the lack of recognition or financial recompense can discourage people from becoming trustees. In a society where people have heavy commitments to work and family, the idea of taking on an additional role can be unattractive. This has created an impression that charities face real difficulties when seeking to recruit adequate numbers of trustees to meet constitutional requirements, let alone achieve a sufficient quantity and variety of individuals to deliver the skills, experience and capacity to run a complex modern voluntary organisation. However research by the Charity Commission and NOP (reported in the Commission document *Trustee Recruitment, Selection and Induction*) found that, contrary to common belief, the majority of charities surveyed did not have difficulty recruiting trustees. The research also found that most charities rely on a very limited range of recruitment techniques and the Commission concluded that if charities employed a wider variety of methods, difficulties in recruiting new trustees would be reduced.

## Methods of recruitment

1 *Word of mouth.* Historically, charities have tended to recruit new trustees by word of mouth. Depending on the nature and reputation of the charity, this can be an effective means of recruiting a sufficient number of trustees but risks resulting in a board of people from similar professional and personal backgrounds, lacking the diversity of skill or experience that can be so beneficial for board debate. It may lay the charity open to charges of cronyism.

2 *Networking with other charities.* The not-for-profit sector can be very incestuous, with staff, volunteers and trustees moving between charities. Charities in search of trustees may seek recommendations and references from other charities operating in the same geographical region or area of work.

3 *Trustee brokerage agencies.* There are a number of options for charities wishing to recruit beyond the current trustees' immediate circle of friends and acquaintances. There is now a range of local and national trustee brokerage agencies, working rather like recruitment agencies and volunteer bureaux. These agencies link individuals who are keen to take on a trusteeship with charities looking for new trustees. Services may be geographically based, e.g. many local volunteer bureaux have potential trustees amongst their volunteers. Alternatively, services may be focussed on a particular board role, e.g. treasurer or company secretary, or they may be more general. Charities recruiting through these means will often be required to give the agency some information about the organisation, the frequency and venue etc. of board meetings and any particular requirements relating to the vacancies, e.g. skills required or any restrictions on appointments. The agency will then link the charity to a possible trustee, giving both the charity and the trustee an opportunity to accept or reject the match.

4 *Employee volunteering.* The recognition of employee volunteering as a valuable means of staff development has provided charities

with another source of trustees, as companies may nominate a member of staff to serve as a trustee as a means of training and developing the skills of that staff member.

5 *Advertising.* Another option now frequently used by large charities is to advertise for new trustees as they would advertise to fill staff vacancies. This includes placing advertisements in the national press. This route is also available for smaller charities through the free or reduced cost advertising space available for voluntary groups in some local papers.

6 *Succession planning.* Many organisations are extremely alert to the difficulties of recruiting new board members and have developed structures within the charity to ensure adequate succession of trustees, particularly honorary officers. This may take the form of a dedicated sub-committee the function of which is the recruitment, selection and training of new trustees. More commonly, charities may use sub-committees, consultations, policy development or evaluation mechanisms as means of drawing into the governance of the organisation a range of people, often members of the organisation, who may later go on to join the board. For example, members or service users may be invited to sit on a sub-committee considering different aspects of service development. Such individuals may, through this experience, develop an interest in the governance of the organisation or become more confident about participating in formal meetings and subsequently decide to join the board.

Whatever the method of recruitment, charities should prepare appropriate information for prospective trustees and adopt a selection procedure to filter out those who, for whatever reason, would be better employed elsewhere in the organisation. Before appointment, potential trustees should be aware of the legal responsibility and the scale of the workload that they will be adopting. The charity should be confident that the prospective trustee will be a legally valid appointment who will make a useful contribution to the board. In particular, the charity should identify any skills or experience that are lacking from the current board, e.g. a trustee with business background or operational experience, and the dynamic of the board. The Charity Commission recommends that trustees undertake a skills audit of the board to identify any gaps in the essential skills required.

Charities should, however, be wary of adopting a tokenistic approach to board recruitment by selecting, for example, one lawyer, one accountant, one personnel expert, etc. Rather they should aim to recruit a mix of trustees who will work well as a team, with every team member making a useful contribution. One means by which charities can provide information to potential trustees is through seminars or workshops for candidates on the role of the trustee in general and within the organisation. This may have the additional benefit of helping trustees to identify any potential conflicts of interest prior to appointment. Trustee job descriptions also serve to clarify the scope and responsibilities of the role.

**tips**

*Participation workshops.* Hold participation workshops for members, users and others who may be interested in joining the board. At the workshop discuss the structure of the charity and the function of different groups within the charity, looking at the role of the board, any sub-committees and volunteers.

Make the workshop a real and positive experience by inviting existing trustees, committee members and volunteers to give presentations about their work and achievements. Include discussion about responsibilities, time commitments and the level of support available for trustees, committee members and volunteers, encouraging people to decide which role best suits them. Those keen to see instant results may be better involved as volunteers rather than on the board, where it can take some time for decisions to filter through implementation to end results.

The session should be timed before nominations are required for the AGM and election of the board, but not so far in advance that potential trustees get distracted by other issues and lose interest.

*Open board meetings.* Hold an open board meeting so that members and potential trustees can see how the board functions. Alternatively, invite potential trustees to attend a normal board meeting.

## Appointment

Not everybody can serve as a trustee and it is in the interest of the charity and the trustees to ensure that all potential trustees are legally entitled to hold that role prior to appointment.

## Disqualification

Some people are disqualified from serving as charity trustees. People in
the following circumstances cannot serve as charity trustees.

1 Those under the age of 18.
2 Undischarged bankrupts.
3 Those who have made compositions or arrangements with
   creditors that have not been discharged.
4 Those who failed to make payments under an administration order
   imposed by the court (the precise details of this disqualification are
   complex and trustees who are concerned that it may apply should
   seek further information and advice as appropriate).
5 Those with unspent convictions for offences involving deception or
   dishonesty (this includes convictions for theft and fraud).
6 Those who, due to misconduct, have been removed from a
   trusteeship by the Charity Commission or a court in England,
   Wales or Scotland.
7 Those who have been disqualified under company law from acting
   as a company director.

Under company law, orders may be made disqualifying the following
people from becoming a company director or taking part in the
formation, promotion or management of a company.

1 Those with a conviction for an indictable offence involving the
   promotion, formation or management of a company.
2 Those who have repeatedly breached requirements to provide
   information to the Registrar of Companies.
3 Those with a conviction for failure to supply information to
   Companies House.
4 Those who have acted fraudulently in winding up a company.
5 Those involved in wrongful trading and failing to pay under a
   county court order.
6 Those considered unfit to serve as a director (e.g. following an
   investigation or when a director's conduct with an insolvent
   company renders the director unfit).

It is an offence for an undischarged bankrupt to serve as a company
director.

These restrictions are relevant to all charities, as an individual who is
disqualified from acting as a company director cannot serve as a charity

trustee. They are also relevant to companies limited by guarantee which are not registered charities.

It is an offence to act as a trustee whilst disqualified. Those disqualified from acting as trustees should not seek appointment to charity boards and, if they become disqualified whilst serving as a trustee, must resign their membership of the charity's governing body. Charities are advised to alert potential trustees to the requirements in terms of disqualification. Existing trustees who are involved in the appointment of a disqualified trustee are likely to be acting in breach of trust.

A person disqualified from trusteeship may apply to the Charity Commission for a waiver which will allow him or her to serve as a trustee of an unincorporated charity.

The governing document may also impose requirements in relation to eligibility to stand as a trustee. For local charities, the constitution often requires that the trustees should live or work within the charity's area of benefit. User organisations may require that all trustees are users of the charity's services.

## Election or appointment?

Governing documents usually determine whether trustees take their board role through election or appointment. Elected boards obviously offer the democratic route with accountability to the electorate. In some organisations, this route is neither appropriate nor possible: for example, where there is no membership.

Although election is often the preferred method of appointment, especially in charities with a large membership, it can present problems in filling identified gaps in the board, whether these are related to a skills shortage or lack of demographic diversity. Charities often seek to address these problems by informing the electorate of the gaps and trusting them to make appropriate appointments. If this method is not used or not useful, most governing documents allow boards to co-opt a number of trustees, often with full voting rights.

Where the only available method of bringing in new trustees is appointment, it may be beneficial for a body other than the existing trustees to be able to make a small proportion of the appointments, provided that this will not undermine the charity's independence. Boards solely appointed by the existing trustees run the risk of perpetuating inequalities or a lack of diversity on the board, particularly where trustees recruit in their own image. At best, such appointment systems may foster cronyism, at worst they may allow trustees to appoint others who will collude in any ongoing impropriety.

Many boards include reserved places for nominated or representative trustees, such as those appointed by a local authority or user group. Such trustees, the board as a whole and, most especially, the nominating or represented body, should be alert to the responsibility that all trustees share to act in the best interests of the charity, rather than the body which they represent or were nominated by. All trustees should be clearly informed of their responsibilities before appointment, but it is particularly important in this case as new trustees may soon find themselves in a position of conflicting loyalties, which they will need to manage as a conflict of interest.

---

## CHECKLIST – PROSPECTIVE TRUSTEES

Prior to appointment trustees should know:

- ☑ trustees' responsibilities, both general and legal (this may be best communicated through the Charity Commission leaflet *Responsibilities of Charity Trustees*);
- ☑ the job description for the role of trustee;
- ☑ any additional job description for the specific role, e.g. treasurer or secretary;
- ☑ limitations on trustee appointments;
- ☑ level of commitment required by the charity;
- ☑ information regarding conflicts of interest;
- ☑ the charity's expenses policy;
- ☑ frequency, timing and venue of board meetings; and
- ☑ the activities of the charity and the key issues it faces in the coming year.

---

It is good practice for charities to confirm the appointment of new trustees and to ask trustees to literally 'sign up' to the charity. This may include signing any code of practice that may have been developed by the charity for the trustee board; signing the organisation's confidentiality and/ or equal opportunities policy; and completing any declaration of interests.

Companies House must be informed of the appointment of new directors within 14 days of the appointment. Forms are available from Companies House for this purpose. Details of newly appointed directors should be added to the company's register of directors and if the director has any interests in the company's contracts these should be recorded.

---

**tip**

**Trustees' Code of Practice**

New trustees may be required by the charity to sign up to a code of practice. This may include:

- a commitment to act in the best interests of the charity;
- adherence to internal policies, such as confidentiality, equal opportunities and health and safety;
- a commitment to attend a minimum number of board meetings per year;
- the conduct expected during board meetings;
- a commitment not to bring the organisation into disrepute; and
- a declaration of interests and a commitment to declare any interests that arise in future.

---

## Induction

All organisations should provide a structured induction programme for new trustees, even if extensive preparatory work was undertaken prior to appointment if or an individual has served as a trustee before. The purpose of the induction is to ensure that trustees have a basic competence in all areas of their role and to ensure that they understand the activities and structure of the charity and their function within the charity. It also supports trustees in adapting to their role and helps them to play an active part in the organisation's governance from an early stage in their trusteeship.

The induction process should cover the following key areas:

- a brief history of the charity and the context in which it currently operates;
- the organisation's legal structure, including a copy of the governing document, information on key areas of interest for trustees and copies of any bye-laws or standing orders;
- information on the role and responsibilities of trustees generally and in relation to the charity;

- details of the governance, management and staffing structure, including contact details for all trustees and key staff;
- information on trustee meetings, including frequency, format, content, copies of minutes for the last few meetings and dates for future meetings;
- the latest set of annual accounts and the annual report;
- the latest management accounts, an overview of the charity's financial situation, suitable training in understanding the accounts and guidance on the key points to be mindful of when reviewing accounts;
- any relevant policies of the charity, e.g. equal opportunities, confidentiality etc;
- a thorough overview of the activities of the charity;
- any recent monitoring or evaluation reports; and
- a digest of key issues facing the charity.

Obviously a lot of this information will be paper based, but giving a new trustee a huge file of paperwork is not an adequate form of induction. There can be no guarantee that trustees will read or understand the papers and it is not the most engaging way of communicating information. However appropriate documents, such as the governing document, list of other trustees, accounts etc. should be supplied as 'compulsory reading' with access to further information for reference purposes and to support other methods of induction.

Given the volume of information to be communicated to new trustees, it may be desirable to use a variety of methods in different sessions so that trustees remain engaged and are active participants in the process, retaining the information communicated.

Many charities run induction days for new trustees. These may include presentations on the trustees' role and the charity's work. Such sessions provide opportunities for new trustees to meet existing trustees, key staff, volunteers and service users. It can also be useful to bring in external speakers to cover areas such as the role of trustees, finance training or the wider context within which the organisation exists. Alternatively, any internal induction could be complemented by sending trustees on external courses provided by the local Council for Voluntary Service or another appropriate training provider.

For larger charities and those providing direct services, it can be very useful for trustees to visit different premises or activities of the charity in order to see the charity in action. This may be arranged as part of a trustee's ongoing training as well as his or her induction as it helps to emphasise the end result of the trustee's work and to build a connection between the trustees and the service users and operational staff.

Once the initial introductory stage of induction has been completed, charities may wish to offer continuing support to new trustees, for example by pairing a new trustee with a more experienced trustee who will be available to explain procedures and documentation or fill in background information and answer questions if necessary. This form of 'buddying' could be time limited or ongoing, but charities should be aware of the risk that prolonged buddying or mentoring relationships can develop or perpetuate factions in the board. An alternative may be to have one board member, e.g. the vice chair or secretary, who takes responsibility for the induction of all new trustees. Whoever takes on this support role, it is essential that all the existing trustees have a clear understanding of the charity's purpose and their role as trustees, so that misconceptions are not perpetuated in the new generation of board members.

**tip**

**Induction logs**

Give each new trustee an induction log. This may take the form of a checklist on a sheet of paper or a more detailed folder.

The log should include a list of all the areas you expect trustees to cover during the induction period. Trustees should sign and date each item as it is completed. Ideally, space should be provided for trustees to comment on the different elements of the induction programme. These comments can then be used to adapt any future induction programmes to better suit the needs of new trustees.

Induction logs should also provide space for trustees to list any outstanding or future training requirements and identify areas of concern.

The chair of the board should be available to meet with all trustees on an individual basis to address any concerns and identify any future training needs. This is particularly important in the early stages of trusteeship, and regular meetings should be scheduled.

Support for trustees should not end after the induction period. Ongoing training and support is crucial to ensure that trustees have a good understanding of current issues and do not become stale. Such training will help trustees to fulfil their roles effectively and remain engaged with the charity, in turn supporting the retention of board members.

The checklist below may prove useful in supporting new trustees.

## CHECKLIST – TRUSTEE INDUCTION

☑ Does the trustee have a list of forthcoming meetings, including venue details?

☑ Has the trustee been given all essential paperwork (e.g. governing document, annual report, business plan, mission statement, papers for the last and next board meetings, including management accounts)?

☑ Does the trustee have access to other paperwork that may be needed for reference?

☑ Does the trustee have contact details for other board members and key staff?

☑ Has the trustee attended a trustee induction session?

☑ Does the trustee understand his or her responsibilities as a trustee?

☑ Have critical issues affecting the charity been discussed with the trustee (e.g. funding applications, confidentiality requirements)?

☑ Has the trustee visited the premises and met key staff and volunteers?

☑ Has the trustee attended finance training?

☑ Has the trustee signed any required documents (e.g. code of practice, confidentiality policy)?

☑ Has the trustee identified his or her future training needs and have arrangements been made to meet these needs?

☑ Has the trustee met with the chair, following induction, to feedback on the induction process?

### POTENTIAL CHANGES – DECLARING PROCEDURES

As part of its review of charity law, the Cabinet Office Strategy Unit recommended that charities should include a statement in their annual accounts describing their procedures for recruiting, inducting and training trustees.

## Representative trustees and user and carer trustees

Trustees who represent a particular organisation or constituency and those who use the organisation's services or care for a service user may face particular problems when discussing certain issues on the board agenda.

### Conflicts of loyalty and interests

Where trustees have been nominated by a section of the charity or an external organisation or elected by a constituency of the organisation's members they often, understandably, feel that their primary allegiance is to that nominating body or constituency. However the law is clear – a trustee's primary responsibility is to act in the best interest of the charity. This means that such trustees must make decisions in the interests of the charity as whole, even where this may contradict the interests of their nominating body. The same is the case for user and carer trustees. As with all trustees, they must not make decisions in their own interests or disregard the interests of the charity.

In some cases for user and carer trustees there may be a clear, direct and personal conflict of interest, for example if the level of service provision to an individual is under discussion. Here appropriate action should be taken to prevent trustees operating under conflicting interests, i.e. the trustee in question should withdraw from the discussion and the decision. However there will be many other cases where the trustee is affected as one of a group of users or carers and these can be more difficult to manage. For this reason it is important that user, carer or representative trustees are clearly informed prior to appointment and during induction of their obligation to act in the charity's best interest and that this interest extends beyond immediate concerns to include care for the future health of the organisation.

Where it is impossible to reconcile the interests of the charity with those of the users, for example where a charge for services is being considered, some innovative solutions to managing the conflict may have to be considered. This especially true where the board is user led and it is simply not possible for all those with conflicting interests to withdraw, as the meeting would no longer be quorate. Solutions include undertaking a thorough appraisal of the options to be considered and using this as the foundation for discussion. Such an appraisal may be conducted by an independent agency and should consider the impact on the users and the organisation, financially and otherwise, immediate and long term, of each option. This information may assist the trustees in making an objective decision. Another solution may be to draw on the skills of an independent, external facilitator to chair a difficult debate. These options help trustees both to make decisions that are truly in the best interest of the charity and also to demonstrate that they have done so, thus minimising the appearance of a conflict of interest.

## Confidentiality

Another issue that can prove difficult for representative, user, and carer trustees is confidentiality. Often, during the course of trusteeship, trustees will gain information that is confidential to the charity. The nature of this confidentiality may be commercial, i.e. it relates to the work of the charity, or it may be personal information regarding another trustee, a member of staff, volunteer, service user or carer. All trustees should treat such information as confidential, and this is an area that should be covered on induction. Trustees may even be asked to sign a confidentiality statement. It can be a particularly difficult issue for those who are closely involved in the operational aspects of the charity and may have direct connections with the issue at hand. It is essential that such trustees are mindful to act in the best interests of the charity in these circumstances.

## Reviewing the process

There is little value in implementing a comprehensive recruitment, appointment and induction process if you do not consider its effectiveness. The board as a whole should regularly review the process to test whether it has met the required objectives, be they recruiting a certain number of trustees or gaining specific skills or diversity within the board.

See chapter 10 for detailed information on monitoring and evaluation.

# **4**    Structuring the board

## INTRODUCTION

The term 'board structure' conveys images of rigidity and formality, but just as a charity itself will develop in response to the external environment, so should the board – form should fit function, with the board being appropriately structured to meet the changing demands of the charity's governance. This does not mean that boards should be everchanging and fluid, as there needs to be a degree of stability in the organisation's governance, but charities should regularly review whether their board structure is meeting their governance needs. In this chapter we will look at some issues to consider when designing the governance of your organisation.

## Overall structure

### Governing document

The governing document usually prescribes the key elements of the board's structure, including the size of the board (most often in the form of maximum and minimum sizes), quorum and method of appointment. This should be the first reference point when considering the governance structure. Governing documents can be changed, but before changes are made, it is important to consider the reasoning behind the structure determined by the governing document. For example, there may have been valid precepts behind the establishment of a board drawn from regional or divisional groups. These precepts may still stand, or they may have been superseded by a changing context.

### Determining the governance structure

When considering whether the structure is right for your charity, look at the scope of your work – are the different regions, projects or client groups catered for reflected in your board? Does the diversity of your work determine the structure and skills of your board? Do you have a membership to draw from in terms of nominations to the board or the election of board members?

## Size to fit function

Two of the key elements to consider when determining board structure are the constituency or constituencies from which the trustees will be drawn, and the size of the board. These two factors are often incompatible. The problems presented by nominated or representative trustees have been discussed in the earlier chapters of this guide, but there may be valid reasons for drawing trustees from different sections of the charity, for example if aiming to develop a more united and cohesive organisation following a period of internal conflict and division.

Boards drawn from sections within the charity or from other interested organisations tend to be large – some charities with this type of structure can end up with a board of up to 60 people. Boards of this size rarely function effectively as it is impossible for them to make unanimous or consensus decisions or to gel as a cohesive unit. There is a risk of factions developing and it is highly unlikely that the individual members will have any real sense of ownership, resulting in poor attendance and decision making. Small boards can be equally unhealthy for a charity as they, by definition, offer only limited skills and experience. They may not encourage debate and may allow greater opportunities for trustees to collude in acting in their own interests rather than those of the charity. The Charity Commission recommends a minimum of three trustees to help mitigate the risk of collusion.

Organisations should consider the activity of the board, particularly in relation to the size and constituency of the organisation and the amount of work delegated to staff, and create a board where size fits function. A board of between 8 to 12 people provides a balance between the extremes discussed above – an adequate range of skills and experience to promote debate and good decision making, and a group which is small enough to work cohesively in governing the charity.

## Composition of the board

Organisations may develop a variety of approaches to board composition and these are frequently combined within individual boards. For example, board members may be drawn from different sections of the charity (be those regional or project orientated), they may be elected or appointed from amongst the membership or other supporters, or they may be representatives of other organisations. This last scenario is common in local charities, which frequently have representatives of the local authority and the Council for Voluntary Service on their boards.

This 'mix and match' approach means that some boards have different classes of members, e.g. full members with voting rights, associate members without voting rights and co-opted members who may or may not be entitled to vote. If this is the case, the different classes of board members should be clearly defined in the governing document and the trustees should be fully conversant with the distinctions and their own status on the board.

These arrangements of different classes of board member are far from ideal as they can undermine the cohesiveness of the board and create a confused position regarding the legal responsibilities of individual board members. It is preferable if all board members serve as full trustees, with the number of co-opted trustees limited by the governing document to less than one-third of the total board number, with co-opted trustees enjoying full voting rights.

## Diversity and skills

The stereotype of a traditional charity run by men in grey suits still exists, but many charities actively work to develop a diverse board that more accurately reflects society and the charity's end users. Charities may seek diversity on a range of levels, whether these be race, gender, age, disability or professional or social background. Such diversity is encouraged by the Charity Commission and should not be regarded as merely a trend. Diverse boards can be extremely beneficial to a charity as the variety of backgrounds and experience enriches debate. Diversity may also help to establish credibility with certain stakeholders, especially funders and beneficiaries. It is particularly important that charities have access to the appropriate range of skills and experience to run the organisation effectively. Management and financial aptitude and an understanding of the issues with which the charity works are essential to all organisations. Depending on the nature of the charity, further skills such as fundraising or public relations may be valuable. Some charities undertake a skills audit to analyse the full range of skills and experience of existing board members (many of whom may have hidden talents) and to identify any gaps.

Recruitment of trustees with specific skills or backgrounds can be extremely difficult. Targeting advertising or direct approaches to relevant professional bodies, companies or other organisations are all viable options. The situation is more difficult still for charities with elected boards, as there are no guarantees that the membership will elect the candidates most suited to complement the existing board. One approach used by charities in these circumstances is to inform the members of the skills or experience needed on the board and trust them to vote accordingly. The nature of democracy means that this is a far from certain exercise and co-option of trustees can be used effectively to supplement elected posts.

In seeking to achieve diversity, charities should beware of the artificial approach of appointing a representative from each relevant profession or socio-economic group. Although diversity is beneficial for debate, it can also create division. The best board is one that functions well as a team, discussing issues and reaching consensus without unbalanced influence from individual members. A tokenistic approach of appointing a lawyer, an accountant, someone with a disability, someone from a minority ethnic group etc. will not, of itself, create a good board and will be impossible for charities in some regions to achieve, for example where the black and minority ethnic population is very low. Instead, a charity should aim to build a team that is appropriately mixed given its location and client group, and then draw on support from professionals and other agencies as necessary.

---

## CHECKLIST – DIVERSITY ON THE BOARD

A tokenistic or ticklist approach is not suited to ensuring appropriate board diversity or a cohesive governing body. The following list looks at the issues you should consider in order to achieve a balanced board within the context of your location and service.

- ☑ *Race.* Does your board reflect the racial mix of your community and/or users?
- ☑ *Age.* Does your board include a spread of appropriate ages for balance and succession? This is particularly important where the organisation provides

age-related services, e.g. youth organisations would be fairly expected to have representation from young people on the board just as organisations providing services to older people should have appropriate input to their boards.

☑ *Gender.* Is the board mixed and does it need to be? There are cases where a single gender board is entirely appropriate, e.g. women's centres or support groups for male survivors of sexual abuse.

☑ *Socio-economic group.* Does the board reflect the balance of the users and/or the community?

☑ *Users.* Does the board have real experience of the needs of the users of the charity's services, for example through user trustees? Although carers and professionals often claim to understand the needs of users, trustees should be aware that there is often conflict between the parties and as a result carer or professional representation may not only be inadequate, it could be misleading.

☑ *Disability.* Do the arrangements for board meetings facilitate or prevent people with disabilities from participating? Consider issues such wheelchair access, provision of induction loops etc.

☑ *Professional experience.* Do board members have the necessary skills and experience to run the organisation? If not, do they appreciate the limitations of their skills and have access to external advice where necessary?

---

## Continuity vs new ideas

Working in an ever-changing social context, charities need a degree of stability on their boards in order to ensure that the past history of the charity is not forgotten and that organisations are not perpetually buffeted by internal change. Boards can, however, be too stable, becoming stale due to a settled group dynamic and lack of fresh ideas. Board appointment processes can be structured to strike a balance between achieving continuity and bringing in new skills. Such structures also offer the additional benefit of supporting succession to honorary officer posts on the board as there is a gradual turnover of board membership. Often such boards are structured on a three-year cycle, with a third of the board appointed each year and each board member being appointed for a three-year term. This means that, at any point in time, only one-third of board members will have less than one year's experience.

Board members can usually serve a number of successive terms, subject to an upper limit, at which point they may be required to take a complete break from the board.

## Underlying documents

In addition to the governing document, charities need further guidance for the operation of the board and the relationship between the charity and its membership. These documents, be they procedures, policies, standing orders or bye-laws, should fill in the gaps left by the governing document. Although the governing document sets the overall framework for the governance of the organisation, the trustees may need more detailed guidance or a more adaptable approach in some areas. These documents serve to supplement the constitution and as such are easier to amend to suit the changing demands of the charity. They may include: a conflict of interest or confidentiality policy; a procedure for dealing with disputes within the board; bye-laws regarding the conduct of elections; and standing orders regarding membership issues.

Such documents should be valuable at all times, but come into their own at times of uncertainty or dispute by offering a clear, predetermined and fair course of action.

---

**CASE EXAMPLE**

A charity which supported those with disabilities was going through a period of internal conflict. Tensions ran high between the long-standing trustees and those users who wanted greater input into the charity's governance. The different factions each nominated candidates for board elections, and both users and trustees drew staff into the conflict. The bye-laws provided for board elections to be administered by an independent organisation with confidential postal voting. This allowed all members to vote freely and included those who would not have been able to attend the AGM. The process ensured that members, users, and trustees could be confident that the electoral process had been fair and ensured that they respected the final result. This allowed the charity to move forward following the conflict.

## Sub-committees

Sub-committees provide opportunities for charities to consider a wide range of issues in more detail than can be covered in trustee meetings, but there is a risk that the number of sub-committees may multiply and the trustees may lose control of the charity as the sub-committees take on more and more of the board's work. There are a number of ways, however, of using sub-committees positively to contribute towards the governance of the charity without undermining the role of the board and creating undue levels of administration in servicing the sub-groups.

*Terms of reference.* Every sub-committee should have written terms of reference. The broad areas covered by the terms should be common to all the sub-committees and some details should be consistent across all sub-groups. For example, terms of reference should cover the following areas:

- purpose of the committee and anticipated end result or output;
- frequency and/or duration, i.e. standing committee or time or task limited;
- level and scope of delegated authority, e.g. can the committee make decisions and take action in its own right or does it have to refer all recommendations to the board for decision? Does the committee have any delegated budgetary authority and what are the controls on this?
- the composition of sub-groups (the charity may agree be a standard requirement for all sub-committees, e.g. 'the sub-committee must have a minimum of three people and a maximum of eight, of whom the simple majority/at least two members must be trustees of the charity');
- reporting requirements to the full board. This may be another standard detail, e.g. 'every sub-committee must provide a written report to each board meeting or the board meeting immediately after each sub-committee meeting'.

Clearly stated terms of reference relating to the purpose, delegated authority, composition and reporting requirements of sub-committees will help to prevent the proliferation of such committees and to avoid the potential slipping of power from trustees to committees.

*Limited numbers of standing sub-committees.* Many charities have a sub-group to focus on financial and administrative issues e.g. the presentation of accounts, appointment of staff etc. Depending on the charity's work, other sub-groups may be necessary, e.g. charities providing medical or health care may need a sub-group to focus on quality and safety issues.

The number of standing groups should be kept to a minimum, with their purpose and authority clearly defined. There is a risk, particularly with finance sub-groups, that the majority of trustees' power vests with the sub-group rather than the full board. In such circumstances, it may be better for the terms of reference to define the activities of the group in addition to the purpose e.g. 'the group will produce budgets and management accounts for discussion and approval by the board of trustees'.

Additional sub-committees may be established on a task focussed or time limited basis e.g. for the appointment of a new member of staff or the production of a funding application.

Sub-groups do provide an opportunity for charities to draw on a wider range of skills than may be present on the board and to identify and develop the skills of potential future board members.

**Advisory and reference groups**

Charities working in a complex environment may wish to draw on a wider range of skills than is available on the board, but to do this in an ad hoc way, rather than through a formal sub-group. One option is to set up a body of advisors or a reference group that can be called upon either individually or collectively as and when needed. This can be particularly effective for organisations working in scientific or politically complex fields, e.g. environmental organisations or charities campaigning for welfare rights. This can also be a useful way of recognising the skills and contributions of former board members, especially when making the transition from large to small boards.

## Framework for a governing document

Model governing documents for trusts, unincorporated associations and companies limited by guarantee are available from the Charity Commission. These models are useful to all not-for-profit organisations. Those with charitable purposes are advised to use the model documents as a starting point as this will ease the process of applying for Charity Commission registration.

The Charity Commission models include all relevant sections of the governing document, so specimen wording has not been included in this guide. However, the models should not just be adopted as they stand. The models are just that – models – and charities should consider what they require of their governing document before finalising the wording. Some areas of the Charity Commission models are blank, as the exact terms are for decision by the individual charities. It may also be useful to refer to the governing documents of similar groups for suggestions regarding common constitutional elements.

Here we will consider the key areas to be considered, whether writing your organisation's first constitution or revising an existing document.

## Basic principles

*Usefulness.* Before you start work on your governing document and throughout drafting you should keep in mind the purpose of the document as the framework for the charity's governance, the foundation upon which it rests. It should be a useful document that can be referred to in order to answer questions regarding governance, rather like a guidebook for the trustees and the charity's secretary. As such it should be well structured and written in clear and accessible language.

*Flexibility.* Although governing documents can be changed, frequent alterations create uncertainty as well as being administratively burdensome. It is advisable to develop a governing document that has the flexibility to cope with developments in the charity without being so vague as to be meaningless. When drafting the document, consider potential developments within the charity over the next five to ten years. Does the document facilitate or prevent such changes? You should be particularly conscious of whether the area of benefit, objects and powers allow for the expansion of the charity's activities.

*Practicality.* The terms of the governing document should be realistically achievable. This is particularly important when it comes to issues such as the required number of trustees or the quorum for meetings and, again, those drafting the document should consider the potential expansion of the charity in future. Clauses that may seem reasonable now, e.g. an AGM quorum of 10 per cent of members out of a current membership of 100, may be completely impractical in the future should the membership grow to 2,000 people.

Again, a balance is required. In ensuring that the provisions are practical, do not make requirements so easy to fulfil that they leave the charity open to abuse e.g. an AGM quorum of three people.

*Relationship between the governing document and legislation.* Charity and company law establish the foundations on which organisations must run – the default position. Governing documents may require higher, but not lower, standards. This relationship should be considered when drafting the governing document. If the document's requirements are less stringent than the prevailing legislative position, the law will apply; however, if the governing document specifies a higher standard, this must be followed. This can present particular difficulties for charities in relation to, for example, financial reporting requirements, as the legal position may change or the organisation may pass between different thresholds. In this area, some charities have addressed the problem by drafting the relevant clauses to state that the charity will comply with the prevailing legal requirements.

## Key clauses of the governing document

*Name of the charity.* The governing document should be in the full name of the charity. This is often given in the first clause. If the charity is to operate under an acronym or different name, give it here.

*Area of benefit.* Most charities operate within a defined geographical area or 'area of benefit'. When writing this clause, bear in mind that local authority boundaries may change in future and that if the charity operates outside the area defined by its governing document it will be acting ultra vires. Many charities resolve this by avoiding reference to a local authority and instead describe their area of benefit as a certain location and the surrounding area.

*Purpose or objects.* This is the most important element of the governing document as it defines the organisation's raison d'être. For organisations seeking charity registration, the wording of this clause will be one of the key determinants of charitable status, as the objects described must fall within the four heads of charity, as described in chapter 1.

The objects clause cannot be changed without the permission of the Charity Commission so, ideally, it should describe the purpose of the charity throughout its existence. As such it should be broadly worded to describe the overall aims of the organisation rather than the methods of achieving those aims, as these are likely to change during the life of the charity. For example, the objects could be simply to promote the welfare of those suffering from a particular type of illness. Sometimes the objects and area of benefit clause may be combined, e.g. 'to promote the welfare of people with mental ill health living or working in Greater Manchester and the surrounding area'.

Charities may have multiple purposes and the objects clause can be much more detailed than the example given above.

When an organisation is committed to a particular model of work and this is part of the purpose of the charity (as is the case with user groups) this may be included within the objects clause.

The objects clauses of registered charities can be viewed on the Register of Charities via the Charity Commission website at www.charity-commission.gov.uk. This can provide useful examples of suitable object clauses which may be adapted by new charities.

*Powers.* This section of the document defines the things that the charity can do in order to achieve the objects. It should be separate from the objects clause and should not focus on the activities of the charity but on the broad authorities given to trustees and should include:

- power to employ staff;
- power to own or lease property;
- power to raise funds;
- power to borrow money;
- power to invest funds.

Trusts and incorporated associations should also include a power to change the organisation's name. This is not necessary for companies limited by guarantee as changes can be made by members' resolutions.

Again, it is important to be forward looking when determining the powers. Powers that may seem superfluous now could be essential in future years.

If seeking charitable status, be careful not to include powers that are not charitable, such as the distribution of profits to members.

*Membership.* If the charity is to have a membership, this should be described in the governing document. This is essential in the case of a company limited by guarantee, as it is the membership that provides the guarantee.

The governing document should explain how people are admitted into and removed from membership, any different classes of members, voting rights and, if appropriate, the maximum number of members. Restrictions may be placed on eligibility for membership, but these should not be discriminatory and should be appropriate to the charity. It would, for example, be acceptable to restrict membership to those living in the area of benefit or suffering from the illness that is the focus of the charity's work.

There may also be a clause limiting the extent to which members may benefit from the charity, e.g. 'members may not receive a share in any surplus'.

*Board of trustees.* As has been discussed elsewhere in this chapter, the structure of the governing body should be determined by the governing document. This should include the number of trustees, the method of appointment and retirement, removal or resignation, the minimum number of meetings per year and the procedures and quorum for trustee meetings. The number of trustees is normally expressed as minimum and maximum with the quorum (i.e. the minimum number of trustees that must be present for a meeting to be valid) described as a proportion of the board or a minimum number, whichever is greater. The governing document should also include arrangements for the resignation of trustees, including the minimum number that can remain after resigna-tions; i.e. a trustee can only resign if there are at least x trustees remaining. As a matter of good practice the minimum number of trustees, the quorum and the minimum remaining trustees should not be less than three. Maintaining a minimum of three trustees reduces the opportunities for abuse. If less than three trustees remain, their powers should be limited to appointing sufficient trustees to restore the minimum number and calling an extraordinary general meeting.

Requirements for the retirement and rotation of trustees should also be included. Indefinite appointments make for stale boards, whereas annual elections offer little continuity. Many charities operate on a retirement/rotation principle, with three-year appointments for trustees and one third of the board retiring each year. Governing documents should include any restrictions on the number of consecutive terms that trustees may serve.

The provisions relating to trustees should also describe the level of benefit that trustees can receive from the charity. As has been discussed in previous chapters, the usual requirement is that none of the trustees should benefit and this should be clearly stated in the governing document. Where payment to trustees for professional services is allowed, this should be specifically included in the governing document, as should any arrangements for the payment of trustee indemnity insurance premiums from charity funds.

*Annual general meeting (AGM).* The governing document should include arrangements for calling and running the AGM, including notice periods, method of delivery of notice, members' resolutions and the quorum. The document should also cover other general meetings, such as extraordinary or special general meetings and the business that must be decided at a general meeting, rather than by the board of trustees.

*Accounts.* Governing documents should give instructions on the control of the charity's bank account and require annual accounts to be produced and presented to the general meeting, often specifying the method of examination. This is an area that charities should be wary of when drafting governing documents as reporting requirements change and charities move between reporting thresholds. Charities may find that their governing document requires an audit, whereas the statutory requirement may be for a less onerous independent examination, but the higher constitutional standard will apply. Charities are advised to draft the clause so that it requires compliance with the prevailing legislation, rather than specifying the method of examination.

*Changes to the governing document.* The governing document should describe the process by which it can be amended. This is normally by a resolution presented to a general meeting. Certain changes to the governing documents of registered charities require Charity Commission approval. These are changes to the objects, amendment and dissolution arrangements, and any provisions authorising trustee benefits, extending investment powers or spending permanent endowments. Charities should either seek Commission approval prior to any of these amendments being made or agree amendments specifying that they are subject to the Commission's approval.

The terms of this clause should be sufficiently stringent to prevent minority factions implementing constitutional change.

Charitable companies do not need to include an amendment clause as companies legislation lays down the procedure for changing memorandum and articles of association.

If the governing documents of unincorporated organisations do not include any power or provision to make amendments, registered charities may apply to the Charity Commission for an order or scheme. The Charity Commission will make an order to give trustees administrative powers that are not currently available in the governing document. This can be done quite swiftly. In contrast, a scheme directly changes the constitution. This is a time consuming process involving two periods of public notice of the constitutional change. Clearly it is preferable for charities to include an appropriate amendment clause. Organisations which are not registered may have no alternative but to wind up, establish a new group and transfer the assets across.

*Dissolution.* Governing documents should include provision for the closure of the charity. This may occur if the charity has achieved its purpose, become redundant due to social, political or economic change, has inadequate support to operate, or is no longer financially viable. The governing document should describe the process of closing the charity (normally through a general meeting) and the distribution of any funds remaining once liabilities have been met. The normal requirement is for the remaining assets to be passed to another organisation or multiple organisations with similar objects to the closing charity. Some registered charities do not have a dissolution clause; however the requirements of charity law ensure that any remaining funds are appropriately allocated to similar charities.

---

**PROPOSED CHANGES – NEW FORM OF INCORPORATION AND TRUSTEE REMUNERATION**

The Cabinet Office Strategy Unit has recommended that a new legal structure be developed exclusively for charities – the Charitable Incorporated Organisation (CIO). Should this proposal be implemented, the Unit has also recommended that model constitutions for CIOs should be available and arrangements should be in place to ease the transition from other legal structures.

The Unit has also recommended that there should be a statutory power for boards to remunerate individual trustees for services they provide to the charity over and above their trustee role.

---

## Group structures

Approximately 27,000 charities in England and Wales are classified by the Charity Commission as branches or subsidiaries of another charity and many not-for-profit organisations operate within some kind of group structure. Where such structures are formally constituted, the roles of the trustees will be slightly different from that of trustees in independent charities. In this section, we will look at the role of trustees of organisations that fit within a wider structure, be they local or national organisations.

### Different types of group structure

1  *Informal.* Charities may as well have invented the term 'networking'. Although some areas of charity work may be jealously guarded, whole infrastructures exist to facilitate the sharing of information and experience. Sometimes these structures may be led by a dedicated organisation, such as a council for voluntary service, but in many cases it is simply that a number of charities which share a common agenda combine to share information, problems and solutions. These structures may have a formal element, such as local charities being the legal members of a council for voluntary service, affiliation fees to an umbrella body or a formal contract for support services, but few of these informal structures significantly affect the role of individual trustees.

2  *Dependent branch.* These may be set up by a parent body or independently established but later join the parent organisation. Commonly, the parent organisation will be national or regional with local branches. Although exact features vary, dependent branches usually share the charity number and governing document of the parent body. They might not have a separate bank account and their accounts are likely to be included within those of the parent organisation. The trustees of the parent organisation will act as trustees for the whole organisation, with local boards functioning more as sub-committees of the parent board, although there is unlikely to be any parent representation on the local committee. These structures can be cumbersome and challenging to govern, particularly if there is a large number of branches, as it can be difficult for the trustees to monitor the local activities and finances for which they are ultimately responsible, making financial reporting particularly complex. Branches under this type of structure often have very limited functions, for example fundraising for the parent body.

3 *Independent branches.* Like the dependent branches, these may be established locally or by the parent body, but independent branches will be separately constituted with their own governing document, bank account and annual accounts. The branch trustees will be independent of the parent trustees although the organisation is likely to have to operate within a framework determined by the parent body in order to use its name and logo. These structures often operate like a form of franchise, with the local branch paying a fee to the parent body for use of the name and logo and any additional support offered by the parent. The parent may place certain requirements on the branches, for example regarding the wording of the objects clause, the range of activities undertaken and the standard of service offered. Local trustees operate as full trustees of their branch with the additional responsibility of conforming to the requirements imposed by the parent body. Local trustees often form the board of the national body and this can present the problems of representative trusteeship as discussed in this and previous chapters. The independence of the branches can make it very difficult for parent bodies to control the structure as a whole. The ultimate sanction is to withdraw from a local branch the right to use the charity's name and logo.

4 *Group structures.* Group structures occur where a number of organisations link together as a consortium, sometimes forming another, separate, entity. Such structures tend not to be hierarchical, with all members of the group having equal status, more akin to a sibling relationship than the parent/branch arrangement of the other formal groups, although one member, or the separately constituted entity that is the group, may provide administration services for all. Common in the corporate sector, these structures are popular amongst housing associations in the not-for-profit sector and may be the forerunner to a merger of a number of organisations.

## Who is responsible for what?

The respective responsibilities and authorities of trustees can easily become confused in branch and group structures and it is important for trustees to seek clarity on this issue. Where responsibilities are ill defined, there is a real risk of them not being met. Documents that define the responsibility of parent and branch trustees and the level of branch trustees' authority and liability should be in place. Any branch structure should also have a disputes procedure for resolving conflict between local groups and the parent body.

The primary indicators that identify whether branches are dependent or independent are their governing documents and their charity or company registration. Separate governing documents and separate registration with the Charity Commission and/or Companies House are strong indicators that organisations operate as independent branches.

The exact structure of a charity also has a bearing on the presentation of its accounts. For further information, see chapter 7.

# **5**   Running the board

---

## INTRODUCTION

One of the most common reasons for difficulties within charities is the poor
functioning of the board. This may happen for a variety of reasons, possibly
because trustees do not fully understand their role or because the members of
the board do not work effectively together. Although such problems are often
attributed to personality clashes, conducting meetings effectively can do much to
overcome the trickier elements of group dynamics and ensure that all board
members are able to participate fully.

---

## Why meet?

Negative experiences of meetings can leave some people feeling that
meetings are a fruitless inconvenience that interrupts the 'real' work. Yet
meetings are crucial for charity trustees as they provide the principal
means for collectively governing the charity. Without board meetings,
charities could be victim to unilateral decision making by the chair or
another member of the board, or receive mixed instructions from
individual trustees. Although a degree of governance can be conducted by
phone, letter and e-mail, individual communication does not generate the
same level of debate as meeting as a group. Collective discussion allows
people to bounce ideas off each other and develop arguments. As all
trustees are bound by board decisions, it is preferable for decisions to be
made by consensus rather than majority view, so on contentious issues
meetings are essential in order to agree a decision with which all board
members are comfortable.

In organisations with many different stakeholders and a high level of
public interest, such as charities, making governance decisions through
meetings ensures a level of confidence in the integrity of the board and
provides opportunities for greater openness. For example, interested

parties can be invited to attend or contribute to board meetings and minutes can be circulated to staff.

## Structure and protocol of board meetings

The governing document and supporting papers are the foundations that determine, for example, the frequency of meetings and rules regarding non-attendance. They may also lay down some framework structure for board meetings or specify items, such as financial reports, that must be considered. These documents represent the minimum standard, with trustees being able to increase the frequency of meetings if appropriate.

Structure is essential to make a meeting worthwhile, and this may be shaped to suit the objectives of the meeting and the culture of the board. It may take the form of a predetermined agenda, bullet points on a flip chart agreed at the beginning of the meeting, or discussion of a single issue. Boards may move between different structures at different stages of development or for different purposes. For example, a planning meeting may be very informal to allow the group to gel and to give them the opportunity to think freely. In contrast, a trustee meeting following the award of a new grant may be very formal and structured in order to focus on the development of new work funded by the grant and move ahead as swiftly as possible. Without structure, meetings are likely to run off course and be unproductive.

### Different types of board

Boards operate in different ways. For the sake of illustration, the following section will look at two fictitious caricatures at either end of the spectrum. The extremely formal 'Madam Chairman' board and, at the opposite end, the highly informal 'shorts and sandals' board.

Protocol, like structure, is likely to depend on the culture of the board and the purpose of the meeting. It is common for boards to direct comments through the chair, but some organisations work on a very formal 'Madam Chairman' basis whilst others are very much on first name terms. Similarly, although some boards will vote on all decisions, others will simply get a sense of consensus, confirm the decision and move on. Boards will also have different approaches to discussing agenda items, from formally presented papers, through workshop type-sessions

**BOARD EXAMPLES – TWO EXTREMES**

**'Madam Chairman'**
*Looks like:* Smartly dressed, white, middle aged and middle class board members, consisting of the great and the good. Refer to fellow trustees by their titles, either personal or role related (i.e. Dr Smith, Madam Chairman, etc). Meetings stick rigidly to a predetermined agenda, and are extremely business like. Trustees sit around a board table with Madam Chairman at the top, the secretary on one side and treasurer on the other. Discussion is very formal and the board takes a very conservative approach.

*Most frequently found:* Long standing charities, usually with lots of money.

**'Shorts and sandals'**
*Looks like:* Casually dressed individuals of any class or race. Board members on first name terms only and often with no defined roles within the board but instead function on a co-operative basis. Members sit wherever they like and debate issues passionately, but as there is no agenda, discussion is frequently at a tangent to board business. Tend to be innovative and creative.

*Most frequently found:* Student unions, embryonic groups.

to informal discussion. Again the most appropriate format will depend on the item and board culture. 'Madam Chairman' boards will feel no more comfortable sitting on the floor with a flip chart pad than a 'shorts-and-sandals' board will feel at home with men in suits giving PowerPoint presentations.

Of course, Madam Chairman and shorts-and-sandals boards are extremes, with most boards occupying the middle ground between. Although some tend more to formality and others to informality, boards will adopt different styles depending on the size of the organisation or of the board, the item under discussion and the culture set by the chair or the history of the charity. Membership of the Madam Chairman board is unlikely to be particularly enjoyable or innovative whilst the shorts-and-sandals board may be cripplingly unproductive. The ideal balance for most organisations is to have enough formality to identify the tasks in hand and get the job done, together with sufficient informality to allow people to relax and contribute to the discussion, to foster wide thinking and to allow them to enjoy their roles.

## Planning meetings

### Agendas

Whether it consists of bullet points on a flip chart or a formal list sent out a week in advance, every board meeting needs an agenda. Agendas are crucial to ensuring that each board member knows and shares the purpose of the meeting and that decisions are made on the issues that are most pressing for the charity at that point in time. Every board member should also be able to contribute items to the agenda, usually by identifying items to the chair or secretary in advance of the meeting. Agendas that are distributed before the meeting allow trustees opportunity to prepare for the meeting, thereby improving debate and increasing the value of the meeting.

As well as structuring the meeting, well-designed agendas send out important messages about the relative importance of the issues facing the charity. Most agendas include standard items such as approving the minutes of the last meeting, discussing any matters arising from those minutes and financial reports. The remainder of the agenda is usually determined by the board and the sequence of those items on the agenda can indicate the importance of the issues. Some charities dispense with the routine issues first and leave key items towards the end of the meeting. Whilst there is a degree of logic in this approach in that it allows simple questions to be swiftly dealt with, it can mean that later agenda items are not fully discussed. This is particularly the case where timing for the meeting is tight, where some of the trustees have to leave early, or where the meeting takes place in the evening, as is often the case with charity boards as many trustees are working during the day. As a result, trustee numbers may be dwindling and the remaining trustees tiring just as critical issues are discussed. Possible solutions may be to either place the crucial item higher on the agenda, arrange a dedicated meeting to discuss that one question, or dispense with routine items until a later meeting. The charity secretary and the chair should consider the relative importance of the agenda items. Which is more important to a charity facing an immediate funding or staffing crisis – addressing the crisis and maintaining the existence and activities of the charity, or agreeing the minutes of the last meeting?

A useful tool is to include timing within the agenda. As well as focussing the mind and helping to keep the meeting on track, including a timescale for each agenda item indicates the relative importance of that agenda item. Ideally, meetings should last no longer than two hours. Although concentration waivers long before this point, after two hours tiredness sets in. The starting point is to determine the anticipated length of the meeting. If the meeting is likely to continue for more than two hours, include a break for refreshments and a change of environment before resuming. Within your anticipated timescale, break down the meeting into timing chunks for each item. Standard items such as apologies and the minutes of the last meeting should be brief, whereas discussion of key issue such as a new project, a funding application, or policy development may require 30 minutes to an hour. Timing may be described by the actual time you expect to start and finish each topic or, as in the sample agenda below, in terms of the number of minutes for each item.

---

### SAMPLE AGENDA

*Anycounty Children and Families Forum*
**Board of Trustees**
13.5.200X
7 p.m. at Anycounty CVS, Anytown
Agenda

| | | |
|---|---|---|
| **1** | Welcome | 5 min (*standard item*) |
| **2** | Apologies for absence | 5 min (*standard item*) |
| **3** | Minutes of last meeting (15.3.200X) – papers enclosed | 5 min (*standard item*) |
| **4** | Matters arising | 5 min (*standard item*) |
| **5** | Local authority plans for charging policy – papers enclosed | 30 min |
| **6** | Gaps in childcare provision – papers enclosed | 30 min |
| **7** | Development of new family support service, progress report– papers enclosed | 10 min |
| **8** | Finance report – papers enclosed | 10 min (*standard item*) |
| **9** | Sub-committee reports – papers enclosed | 10 min (*standard item*) |
| **10** | Any other business | 5 min (*standard item*) |
| **11** | Date of next meeting – 17.7.200X | 5 min (*standard item*) |

(It may be useful to add the name of the person leading each item to the agenda)

---

## Papers

As can be seen from the sample agenda, the discussion of many items will be based around papers circulated before the meeting. Some papers may be for information only, intended to generate discussion without necessarily expecting any conclusions or decisions at the meeting. Where a decision is needed, papers should describe the issues for discussion, the options available for decision and the implications of each decision, with a recommended course of action for the board. Such papers help to direct discussion and ensure that an actual decision is made.

Ideally, papers should be circulated in advance of the meeting to allow trustees time to read them and consider the issues raised, formulating any further questions they may have and identifying any options not considered in the paper. Where this is not possible, papers may be tabled at the meeting, but this should only be used as a last resort.

## Timing

On a large or diverse board, it will be very difficult to plan meetings at a time to suit everyone, but it is important to arrange meetings that can accommodate as many board members as possible and do not leave individuals marginalised. When arranging meetings, consider both the professional and domestic responsibilities of board members and their personal circumstances. If trustees have full-time jobs, plan meetings around their working hours and travelling time. Those with young children may prefer meetings during the school day or later in the evening when they can arrange child care. People with disabilities or ill health may need to fit meetings around domiciliary care or medication requirements or may wish to schedule meetings for the time of day when they feel at their best.

Evening meetings often suit trustees who work during the day but these may not be ideal as the trustees are likely to be tired. If evening meetings are essential, they should be kept to an agreed time limit. Another issue to consider with evening meetings is the transport arrangements for trustees and their personal safety when travelling to and from the meeting.

## Venue

The venue should be accessible to trustees, both in terms of geographic location and access into and within the building, particularly if the trustees include persons with disabilities. Geographic location is particularly important for charities covering a large or rural area. It can be a source of friction within boards if the meeting venue continually favours one group of trustees over others, so it is desirable to seek a central venue or one with good transport links so that access is easy for all trustees. Alternatively, meetings may be rotated between a number of different venues. This is useful if the charity operates from a number of sites as it allows the trustees to view the different elements of the charity's work and to meet staff and volunteers.

The venue should be physically accessible to wheelchair users and include appropriate adaptations for other disabilities (e.g. induction loops) to ensure that all those who currently serve on the board or those who wish to do so in future will be able to participate fully in meetings.

Meeting venues should also be comfortable and appropriate for board meetings. There should be adequate space for board members to sit around a table, with separate rooms for refreshments or break-out groups if necessary. Rooms should be well-lit, warm and ventilated.

## Running the meeting

It is the role of the chair to ensure that the meeting is productive. Many problems within board meetings are due to poor chairing. It may be that the chair rules the meeting and stifles debate, allows others to dominate or fails to keep the meeting to the agenda. Keeping control of the meeting means ensuring that everybody is able to contribute to the debate equally, without individuals or a small group dominating to the exclusion of others. The chair should also ensure that the debate is relevant to the item at hand and that discussion is not diverted to superfluous issues.

Chairs of charity boards need to be particularly aware of the 'lowest common denominator effect'. This involves trustees debating the minutiae of an agenda item, such as what colour to paint the office walls, whilst missing the bigger, more difficult issues, such as the development of the charity following the refurbishment. This often happens because trustees feel overwhelmed by the volume or complexity of issues facing them, so find it difficult to prioritise or grasp the more complex challenges. As a result they focus on the details that they can all understand, i.e. the lowest common denominator. It is the chair's role to ensure that the big picture is not lost, for example by arranging for complex issues to be explained in a way that is comprehensible to all trustees.

Other difficulties on charity boards are ensuring participation and dealing with disputes. It only takes a few strong personalities on a board for other trustees to feel unable to contribute and the objective of considered collective decision making is lost. Trustees may be silent to avoid a dispute, because they feel that they have nothing to add or because they are wary of asking a stupid question. Some boards adopt the philosophy that 'there are no stupid questions', reflecting the fact that the supposed 'stupid question' is frequently the one that everybody else was thinking but did not dare to ask. Again it is the function of the chair to ensure participation. This may be done by establishing ground rules that underpin every meeting (see box) or by actively asking those who have not yet contributed to the debate for their views. Some chairs do this by asking each trustee in turn if they have anything to add, others by specifi-cally addressing the silent trustees and asking for their comments.

Significant disputes within boards are less common than lack of partic-ipation, but harder to deal with. Again the chair has a crucial role to play in ensuring that all views are heard, that the opinions expressed are relevant to the item under discussion and that the dispute does not get out of hand. Ground rules can be useful for dealing with disputes, but pain-free resolution is largely dependent upon the agitated trustee's respect for the authority of the chair, as it is only the chair that can draw an item to its close. Where disputed items are not subject to time pressures, a cooling-off period may be allowed, deferring the issue to a subsequent meeting to allow for greater investigation of all views expressed. On some issues it may also be appropriate to consult with a wider group, e.g. service users or volunteers, to see if fresh opinions can aid consensus.

---

**tip**

**Ground rules**
Ground rules can be a useful means of controlling board behaviour. They are normally discussed by the trustees and agreed collectively with trustees 'signing up' to the rules. New trustees may be asked to sign up to a set of rules agreed by the existing board.

*Examples:*
Avoid language that could cause offence.
Respect the authority of the chair.
Everyone's opinion is valid and all trustees will listen to the opinions of others.

---

As board decisions are binding on all trustees, it is preferable to reach consensus decisions wherever possible. Ensuring consensus, rather than making majority decisions, can take more time, but it does mean that issues are fully debated.

## Board roles

The classic board structure involves at least three dedicated posts: chair, secretary and treasurer. Many boards have an additional role of vice chair. Collectively these are the honorary officers of the charity. Each has a very distinct function and some charities have developed job descriptions for each role. This both assists potential honorary officers in understanding the post and provides guidance for those trustees in officer roles.

*Chair.* Several aspects of the chair's role are discussed in the paragraphs relating to running the meeting as this is, essentially, the chair's function. The chair is the first among equals on the board. This leadership role includes responsibility for determining the agenda (usually in partnership with the secretary) and steering the meeting to achieve the agenda's objectives. This involves introducing the agenda item, stimulating debate, keeping discussion to the item at hand, ensuring participation, dealing with dispute, offering suggestions and ensuring consensus. Where consensus cannot be reached and a vote is necessary, most governing documents give the chair a second and casting vote in the event of equality of votes. At the conclusion of each agenda item, the chair should summarise the decisions, identify any actions arising from that decision, agree who will be responsible for that action and set a timescale for its conclusion.

In staffed organisations, the most senior employee is usually managed by the chair.

To the outside world, the chair often represents the board and the charity.

*Vice chair.* The vice chair's role is to deputise for the chair in his or her absence. The role often involves other functions, such as working closely with the chair on business to be conducted between meetings, chairing sub-committees etc.

*Secretary.* The secretary sometimes has the most difficult position on the board as his or her primary responsibility is to the probity of the organisation and adherence to the governing document and legal environment, rather than allegiance to the board. Whilst a significant element of this role involves supporting the trustees in working effectively and legally, the cautions given by the secretary can sometimes be at odds with the wishes of the board, making the function something of a thankless task. The functions include working with the chair and senior staff to plan meetings and produce minutes, maintaining necessary documentation, executing the constitutional requirements (e.g. planning the AGM and board elections) and reporting to regulators as necessary.

*Treasurer.* All the trustees share a collective responsibility for the financial health of the organisation, but it is the treasurer who carries out the board's finance function, often in partnership with senior staff and other board members, sometimes within a finance sub-committee. The treasurer's role includes budget setting, controlling and monitoring expenditure, producing management and annual accounts and presenting financial reports to the board and membership.

The proportion of this work that is actually done by the treasurer will depend on the charity. Much of the work will be done by paid staff or

---

**CASE EXAMPLE**

The treasurer of a charitable company limited by guarantee failed to produce annual accounts for two years in succession. Letters sent by Companies House requesting the accounts and later enquiring if the company was still operating were ignored by the treasurer. The company was eventually struck off the Register of Companies. The organisation incurred considerable expense in restoring the company to the Register and engaging accountants to produce financial reports for the organisation. The treasurer admitted responsibility and resigned his position; however the responsibilities of the trustees are collective and the remaining trustees had taken no action regarding the failure to produce accounts. The charity's funders grew concerned about the remaining trustees' understanding of their responsibilities and their ability to manage the finances of the charity. They threatened to withdraw funding unless appropriate action was taken to remedy the deficiencies in financial management. As a result, several other trustees, including the chair, acknowledged their responsibility and resigned from the board.

professional advisers, but it is the treasurer who must supervise the work and support the board in interpreting financial information and making finance decisions.

Other trustees may also have designated roles, such as staff liaison, volunteer recruitment or quality standards. Whatever the roles of individual trustees, boards must continue to act collectively, as the case study above illustrates.

## Group dynamic roles

In addition to the formal roles determined by the structure of the board, trustees are likely to adopt different roles within the group depending on their own personalities and the inter-relationships between them. There is a host of literature on group/team dynamics and their impact on organisational performance. It is not a subject that will be discussed

---

**BELBIN'S MODEL FOR EFFECTIVE TEAM WORKING**

1 *Co-ordinator.* The co-ordinator will define roles and set goals within the team or group. As the person who co-ordinates the work and talents of others, the co-ordinator needs to be respected by the team.

2 *Plant.* The plant is the creative team member who comes up with new ideas.

3 *Shaper.* This is the dynamic, energetic and challenging member of the team.

4 *Resource Investigator.* Extrovert, develops ideas and makes outside contacts, including securing necessary resources.

5 *Monitor Evaluator.* This team member is the realist. Shrewd, prudent and analytical, the monitor evaluator will keep the team grounded by careful consideration of options.

6 *Implementer.* This team worker is also realistic and will make things happen through a practical and task orientated approach.

7 *Completer Finisher.* The completer finisher has great attention to detail, ensuring accurate and timely work.

8 *Team Worker.* This team member is caring, person orientated and prepared to work to other people's ideas.

9 *Specialist.* The specialist brings technical skill and professionalism to the team, rather than organisational loyalty.

here in any great detail; however it is an issue which should be kept
in mind when considering the board, whether reviewing its success
or failure to function, its composition, leadership or tendency to
dispute.

There are various models of team roles, but one of the most widely
used models was developed by Dr. Meredith Belbin in the early 1980s.
Dr Belbin's model identifies nine roles that are needed for effective team
working (see the box on p. 82).

Clearly, some of these team roles naturally lend themselves to formal
board roles. The co-ordinator is often the chair of trustees and the
specialist may be the independent professional adviser. In small boards,
trustees may fulfil more than one role and many boards will function
effectively without giving any conscious thought to group dynamics.
However the model can be extremely useful and may be a valuable tool
for board appraisal.

Board appraisal is discussed at the end of this chapter.

## Minutes

One of the biggest criticisms of meetings is that they involve a lot of
talking, but then nothing ever happens. This should not happen with
well-run meetings where decisions are made and actions identified.
Minutes of meetings provide one of the key means of ensuring that action
follows meetings. Minutes are important on a number of levels. In
recording the principal discussion points and decisions of a meeting they
provide evidence that issues have been properly debated. They also serve
as an aide-memoire to the board and supply essential background information by acting as a historical record of the charity. By recording
action points, minutes also serve as a workplan for the board. Some
charities present their minutes with an 'action' column on the right hand
side of the page, showing what action is to be taken in respect of each
agenda item, the person responsible for that action, and the timescale
required.

The fact that planned actions are recorded in the minutes is, of course,
no guarantee that the action will be taken. Board members must take
individual responsibility for any tasks that are attributed to them and
the board must collectively ensure that the actions proposed are
implemented.

**SAMPLE MINUTES**

*Anycounty Children and Families Forum*

**Minutes of the trustees meeting on 13.5.200X at Anycounty CVS**

**Present:**

| | |
|---|---|
| Mary Allen (Chair) | Alicia Jackson |
| Brenda Starr (Treasurer) | Indira Khan |
| Xavier Michel (Secretary) | George McIntyre |
| Sanjeev Bashir | Hannah Williams |

**In attendance:** Maggie Harris, Anycounty Social Services

1 Welcome
2 Apologies for absence: Tom O'Leary, Sam Weller
3 Minutes of last meeting (15.3.200X): Item 4 – amend **XM**
   third sentence of second paragraph to read 'The
   consultation period will run for three months'.
4 Matters arising: No matters arising not appearing
   elsewhere on the agenda.
5 Local authority plans for charging policy: The trustees **MA, SB and**
   opposed the implementation of a charging policy but **AJ to draft**
   recognised that its introduction was inevitable and agreed **proposals**
   to consult with the wider membership on proposals to **paper by**
   mitigate the effects of charging. Particular concerns were **14.6.200X**
   raised regarding parents of disabled children and the
   possibility that they would not access services because
   of the charges.
6 Gaps in childcare provision: The trustees agreed with the
   analysis of unmet need in terms of childcare provision
   and added to the list the need for services for newly
   arrived asylum seekers. It was agreed to present the
   revised report to the members' meeting in June.
7 Development of new family support service: MH reported
   that an application has been made to the Charity
   Commission for registration; office accommodation has
   been provided in the Social Services family centre in
   Anytown; and the posts of organiser and admin assistant
   were advertised two weeks ago. Response was good,
   with interviews due to take place early in June. MA will be
   a member of the interview panel.

**SAMPLE MINUTES continued**

| | |
|---|---|
| 8 Finance report: BS reported a slight overspend on travel expenses due to additional, unexpected work undertaken this year in attending meetings relating to the charging policy and the new family support scheme. However there were underspends on office costs and a small donation from the local children's clothes shop has led to a small surplus against target budgets for the first month of the financial year. | **BS to prepare accounts by 15.7.200X** |
|     Accounts for the previous financial year are currently being prepared by BS and the accountant and will be presented to the next meeting. | |
| 9 Sub-committee reports: Reports were accepted as presented. Mandy Baker has resigned from the youth action sub-committee due to pressure of exam revision. It was agreed to write to Mandy thanking her for her contribution to the sub-committee. It was also agreed to seek a replacement youth representative. | **MA to thank MB. GM to recruit new member.** |
| 10 Any other business: No other business. | |
| 11 Date of next meeting: 17.7.200X | |

Meeting closed at 8.30 p.m.

---

## CHECKLIST – RUNNING MEETINGS

☑ Date and time    Does the date clash with any major events or religious celebrations?

                        Is the timing of the meeting convenient for the majority of trustees?

☑ Venue    Is the venue accessible to all trustees?

                        Is there adequate space to run the meeting comfortably?

                        Is the layout of the room suitable for a board meeting?

☑ Papers    Have all trustees had an opportunity to contribute to the agenda?

                        Have the agenda, minutes of last meeting, financial reports and any further papers been circulated to the trustees in adequate time for them to prepare for the meeting?

| ☑ At the meeting | Have all distractions been dealt with (e.g. mobile phones switched off?) |
| | Is any necessary equipment in place, e.g. for presentations? |
| | Are refreshments available? |
| | Is the meeting room at a comfortable temperature? |
| ☑ During the meeting | Is discussion being kept to the agenda? |
| | Is everyone able to contribute to the debate? |
| | Are clear decisions being made? |
| | Has follow up action been clearly defined and allocated and a timescale agreed? |
| | Is the meeting keeping to time? |
| | Has a date and venue for the next meeting been agreed? |
| ☑ After the meeting | Have draft minutes been agreed by the chair and circulated to the board within a reasonable time following the end of the meeting? |
| | Have trustees followed up on agreed action points as appropriate? |

## Board appraisal

As the body with overall responsibility for the organisation, it is essential that boards function effectively. Voluntary sector boards are increasingly recognising just how much the quality of their work impacts on the organisation, and so are considering their own performance as well as the external work of the charity.

Board appraisal may have a number of purposes and take on a range of forms. At one extreme, it may be that the board no longer serves the needs of the charity and that the appraisal is part of an entire review of the governance structure; at the other, it may be a regular review of the contribution of individual board members and their function as a unit, used as a means of further developing individuals and improving board performance.

Whatever the format, board appraisal inevitably involves a high level of critical inspection of individual board members, their fellow trustees and the board as a whole. Understandably this can be a difficult process and the whole concept of board appraisal can be challenging for many board members. It is therefore essential that all trustees are committed to the process and that the purpose of the exercise is clearly defined. It can take many months, if not years, of persuasion before the board as a whole feels ready to undertake such an exercise. Given the potential delicacy of the appraisal, it is essential that it is properly planned and executed.

## Timing and purpose

The timing and purpose of a board appraisal are closely linked, as the stage of the charity's development is likely to determine the purpose of the appraisal. However it is not advisable to undertake an appraisal during periods of crisis or conflict within the charity as the trustees are unlikely to agree a common purpose for the appraisal and the process risks deepening, rather than resolving, any conflict. In addition, the appraisal would distract the trustees from the primary purpose of addressing the crisis or conflict. More appropriate options are to conduct the appraisal following the appointment of a new chief executive, election of a new chair, in response to new funding (particularly if this will bring about large growth), a new business plan or some other external or internal factor. The purpose of the appraisal may be to ensure that the board is equipped to govern the charity following change or to plan or implement future developments. Equally, it may be for a more internal aim, e.g. to agree the boundaries between the roles of the board and chief executive or to clarify trustee roles and functions following the election of a new chair. The Belbin model of team roles, described at p. 82, would be helpful in this context.

Whatever the outcome of the decision, the purpose of the exercise should be clear and should determine the content of the appraisal.

## Method

There are a number of methods of board appraisal. The most appropriate in each case will depend on the purpose of the appraisal and, perhaps most importantly, the culture of the board. For example, a board questionnaire would be best suited to a regular review of board function, whereas a detailed examination of the performance of a board laden with strong personalities and complex histories may be better conducted by an independent, external facilitator. A thorough board appraisal exercise may involve a combination of different methods.

## 1 Do-it-yourself or independent consultant?

Perhaps the first question to address once the purpose of the appraisal has been agreed is whether to conduct the appraisal internally or to draw on the resources of an external facilitator or consultant. The table summarises the advantages and disadvantages of both approaches.

Perhaps the key question to ask is: would the board tolerate an outsider's intervention and accept the conclusions expressed or would they disregard any unpopular or difficult opinions? Much will depend on the quality of the independent consultant.

---

### DIY vs INDEPENDENT CONSULTANT

**Do-it-yourself**
Internally managed board appraisals are often led by a sub-group of the trustee board. Although staff may input into the appraisal, they should not lead it.

| Advantages | Disadvantages |
| --- | --- |
| Knowing the issues, the history, the personalities and the desired outcome (rather than the conclusion) so the process can be sensitive to these | Lacks objectivity |
| | Lacks a fresh approach |
| | It may not be possible for people to be completely honest |
| | Labour intensive |
| Maintaining ownership | |
| Maintaining continuity | |
| Low out-of-pocket expenses | |

**Independent, external consultant**

| Advantages | Disadvantages |
| --- | --- |
| Objective | No knowledge of the history of the charity and the personalities involved |
| Fresh approach | |
| New ideas | Board may lose ownership |
| Experience of similar exercises with similar groups | May not be able to ensure implementation |
| Facilitates honesty and openness | Can be expensive |

## CHECKLIST – CHOOSING AN INDEPENDENT CONSULTANT

The correct choice of independent consultant is essential if an appraisal is to be successful. In selecting a consultant, charities should make their selection from a number of individuals or organisations, with particular attention to the following.

☑ Does the individual have appropriate experience of board appraisal within your type of organisation and circumstances?

☑ Can the consultant give references or recommendations from other voluntary groups?

☑ Does the consultant understand the issues affecting your charity and is he or she sympathetic to them?

☑ Does he or she listen to you?

☑ Do your board members respect the consultant?

☑ Is the method of appraisal proposed appropriate to your board?

☑ Will the proposed content of the process deliver the desired purposes?

☑ Will the consultant present his or her conclusions and recommendations in a manner which is useful to your board?

☑ Will the consultant undertake any follow up work?

---

For boards that seek objectivity in the appraisal exercise but cannot afford the expense of an external facilitator, a compromise solution may be available in the form of a trustee from another organisation undertaking the appraisal. In this way charities can enter into reciprocal appraisal arrangements with like-minded organisations.

### 2 Questionnaires

Questionnaires may be the first point of any appraisal process. These can provide information on areas of concern for trustees that will later form the focus for discussion. Trustees should be given adequate time to complete the questionnaires and arrangements should be made for trustees to complete them anonymously if necessary.

## 3 Group discussions

These stimulate debate as different ideas can be raised and discussed. Group discussions may involve the whole board or small groups. Although some flexibility may be desirable, discussion should be based on an agenda. Such discussions should be conducted separately from regular trustee meetings. Many charities have 'awaydays' or retreats in order to discuss these issues away from daily distractions.

## 4 Individual interviews

These can be a constructive way of identifying the feelings of individual trustees towards the board as a whole and in respect of their own role on the board.

## Conclusion and implementation

Whatever the method of appraisal, the process should end with the preparation of a conclusion. This should include a summary of the findings, interpretation of what these findings mean and proposals for moving forward. Whether the appraisal is conducted internally or externally, the conclusion should be in written form and distributed to the whole board. In many cases, those responsible for the appraisal will also give a presentation of their conclusions. The document and presentation then serve as a starting point for the board to discuss the next course of action. Again, it may be best to have this debate at a retreat or awayday, as this allows time for options to be discussed fully, free from the distractions of other board business.

The board may decide to implement any proposals in their entirety or to take a more selective approach. Whatever the outcome, an implementation and review plan should be developed in order to ensure that the proposals are carried through and the work is not lost. As with all plans, this should look at actions, identify those responsible for each action and set timescales. Where significant changes are being made, due consideration should be given to the impact on all those involved and reviews built into the plan to monitor the progress of implementation and the efficacy of any new systems.

# 6 Trustee–staff relations: roles and responsibilities

## INTRODUCTION

Establishing a healthy working relationship between the trustees and staff is one of the hardest elements of charity management to get right and there are no absolute answers. This chapter looks at some of the problem issues, from recruitment and selection through to dealing with conflict and legal requirements. The legal framework relating to employment is discussed in this chapter, but the application of the law can be complex and specialist advice should be sought on any areas of concern. Personnel management and staff development are beyond the scope of this guide, but the Directory includes suggested reading on these issues.

## Employing staff

The majority of charities start their lives by being run on an entirely voluntary basis, so trustees' roles extend beyond the governance function into day-to-day administrative and operational activities. Often this work is supported by a wider body of volunteers. This method of administration is entirely appropriate for voluntary organisations and many will never move beyond this model. However, for many charities there will come a point when, in order to ensure the survival of the organisation, to uphold the quality of its work or to expand its activities, it becomes necessary to employ paid staff.

### When to employ

The decision to employ a paid member of staff should not be based solely on the availability of funds; rather it should be a strategic choice founded in the wider context of the organisation's maturity, current practice and plans for development. In many cases, charities can function extremely

effectively and for long periods of time supported solely by the effort of
volunteers. This can be a secure and stable method of operation when
work is evenly spread over a large body of volunteers and does not
require huge commitments of time or resources from any of them, but
there is an inherent vulnerability in organisations that are heavily
dependent on a small group of volunteers. Such volunteers are difficult to
replace and the departure of any one of them can have catastrophic
effects on the operation of the organisation. Here the appointment of a
member of staff, for example to undertake administrative duties and co-
ordinate voluntary effort, can bring stability and continuity to the service.
Although individual employees can become just as invaluable to the
organisation as committed volunteers, the paid nature of their role makes
staff much easier to replace.

Even where workloads are evenly spread amongst a large number of
volunteers, many organisations find that there is a limit to what can be
achieved by voluntary work alone and that it is necessary to employ staff
to support any expansion of the service.

Whether staff are to be appointed to maintain or expand the service,
the decision to employ staff should be made not just in the context of a
development plan for the service but also with regard to the maturity of
the board. The appointment of staff has major legal and governance
implications as the trustees will become employers. A board should not
enter this relationship unless the trustees understand the scope and nature
of their legal responsibilities and are able to handle the softer (and often
very tricky) elements of staff management, such as defining boundaries
between board and staff and reviewing performance. It is important for
trustees to have access to appropriate advice and support, whether this be
through paid legal services or through a voluntary sector umbrella body.

In the voluntary sector, the biggest barrier to the employment of staff is
the ability to pay wages. With the exception of endowed charities, most
voluntary organisations will need to fundraise in order to finance staff
salaries. Although large, well established charities may raise significant
sums through tin shaking and legacies, many voluntary sector employers
will be dependent on grant income to cover salary costs. Given the intense
competition for funds, whether sought from statutory bodies, lottery
distributors, corporate foundations or charitable trusts, the charity will
need to demonstrate that the appointment is necessary and that it has the
capacity to recruit and manage staff properly. As a result charities are

often required to undertake much preparatory work in terms of agreeing job descriptions, setting salary levels and initiating appropriate infra-structure changes before funding can be secured.

Perhaps the most important element, whether employing a lone worker or the tenth member of the team, is to determine the exact function of that employee. It is tempting for trustees appointing their first member of staff to identify those aspects of the organisational workload that they like least and delegate this to the worker, retaining their own direct involvement in the more enjoyable elements of operation. This rarely results in an attractive or cohesive post and can lead to difficulties in determining boundaries between staff and trustees. It is far better to identify an element, or appropriate collection of elements, of work that can be delegated to a member of staff without undermining the trustees' governance control.

## Recruiting staff

The first step in any employment process is determining what that member of staff will do. Charities should not appoint just because they need another pair of hands. There should be clear guidelines as to the function of each worker. This may be very obvious in some cases, for example where elements of the charity's work are not being done or where there is a need that is not being met by existing services. On many occasions it is more complex, and it may be necessary to review the operation of the organisation as a whole in order to identify those elements that would be best delivered by a paid member of staff. Issues to consider include whether the employee will:

- have operational responsibility;
- be involved in the direct delivery of services;
- undertake administrative tasks;
- manage other workers or volunteers;
- have a strategic or policy role;
- have any financial responsibility; and/or
- represent the organisation to external bodies and the wider public.

When determining the functions to be carried out by the employee, first consider the skills and experience that will be needed to undertake the role, paying particular attention to whether any one person is likely to possess the full range of skills and experience required. Trustees should be particularly wary of any requirements that are mutually exclusive or

---

**CASE EXAMPLE**

**Problem:** A small community charity had been running a range of services for several years, including a holiday play scheme and a lunch club for older people. The activities were run by the trustees and a group of volunteers. The trustees were struggling with the workload and finding it increasingly difficult to sustain the service. This pressure led to the resignation of a number of trustees, further increasing the burden on the remaining board members. They felt that the appointment of a member of staff would relieve the operational responsibilities of trustees. The service was highly valued by the local authority which indicated that it would make a grant to finance a worker's salary. The trustees were keen to appoint a worker, but remained undecided about his or her exact role.

**Solution:** The trustees reviewed the services offered by the charity and its internal management activities, identifying those areas that were currently causing problems. They then considered which elements could be packaged together to form the job description of the worker. The trustees decided to delegate operational tasks such as the recruitment and co-ordination of volunteers, acceptance of referrals and service delivery to the worker. They also delegated day-to-day administrative duties. However the trustees felt that the recruitment of new board members and compliance with legislation and good practice in relation to the services offered were governance roles and they retained direct control over these areas.

---

otherwise incompatible. It is quite common and reasonable to expect a project manager or lone worker within a small organisation to undertake managerial, administrative, financial and operational functions, but if looking for someone with nursing skills, do not expect that individual to be an accountant, or vice versa. Once these issues have been decided, they should be recorded in the two documents that are critical to the recruitment process, i.e. the job description and the person specification.

## Job description

The term is self explanatory. The job description describes the job. It should give a clear indication to trustees, funders and (most importantly) applicants of the nature and scope of the job. It should include the following information:

- name of organisation;
- job title;
- hours of work;
- rate of pay plus any other benefits, e.g. pension, car, health insurance;
- who the post will be managed by;
- any management responsibilities;
- place of work;
- annual leave entitlement and any arrangements for overtime payments, time off in lieu of overtime payments, or flexitime;
- purpose of the job;
- principal duties: these may give an outline of tasks to be undertaken or include more detail regarding the conduct of the duties, e.g. to work in partnership on particular aspects of the work;
- any ancillary duties.

Job descriptions should be fairly succinct. A job description that extends beyond two sides of A4 gives a fairly clear indication that the job is either too much for one person or that the trustees are being highly prescriptive in determining how the employee should carry out the work.

---

**SAMPLE JOB DESCRIPTION**

*Anycounty Children and Familes Forum*

**Job description**

| | |
|---|---|
| Title: | Co-ordinator |
| Responsible to: | Chair of the Board of Trustees |
| Responsible for: | Administrator |
| Salary: | £22,000 – £26,000 per annum plus 5% pension contribution |
| Hours: | 35 hours per week |
| | Usual office hours: 9 a.m. – 5 p.m. with a lunch break of one hour. |
| | Occasional evening and weekend work required. Time off in lieu of overtime is available. |
| Annual leave: | 25 days per annum, plus bank holidays |
| Place of work: | Anytown CVS, Anytown |

*cont.*

**SAMPLE JOB DESCRIPTION continued**

Purpose:      Responsible for co-ordinating the work of Forum members and volunteers in order to achieve the organisation's aims of improving services for children and families in the county.

**Principal duties:**

1 To represent the Forum to other agencies.
2 To collate information on service provision and developments and present this information to Forum members and relevant third parties.
3 To canvas the opinion of Forum members on relevant issues, developments and documents and present these opinions to third parties as appropriate.
4 To support the development of new services for children and families in the county.
5 To co-ordinate the activities of Forum members through supporting special interest groups and other ad hoc bodies.
6 To assess the training needs of Forum members and arrange training as appropriate.
7 To organise and attend all meetings of the Forum and the board of trustees.
8 To manage the Forum administrator.
9 To report to the board of trustees on a quarterly basis.

**Other tasks:**

1 To prepare the annual report of the Forum, in partnership with the trustees.
2 To take part in fundraising events arranged by the trustees.
3 To compile monitoring information.

**Person specification**

The person specification should describe the skills, experience, knowledge and qualifications required of the employee. Applicants should be able to assess, from reading the person specification, whether they are suitable candidates for the job. Person specifications are normally presented as a table, stating whether the requirements are essential or desirable.

Some organisations also include personal qualities within the person specification. This should only be done where absolutely necessary,

*Anytown Children and Families Forum*

**Co-ordinator – Person Specification**

| | Essential | Desirable |
|---|---|---|
| Skills | Good written and verbal communication skills. Good analytical skills. | |
| Experience | Minimum two years' experience of working in the voluntary sector. Experience of multi-agency work. Experience of working with children and families. Experience of organising meetings and conferences. Compilation of written reports. | Staff management. Arranging training. Monitoring and evaluation of individual pieces of work and/or projects. |
| Knowledge | Legal framework for children and families services. | Service provision in Anycounty. |
| Qualifications | | Recognised professional or academic qualification in relation to the voluntary sector, social care, management, teaching or youth work. |
| Other | Commitment to equal opportunities. | Clean driving licence and access to a car. |

objective and relevant to the post. For example, it may be essential that an outreach worker be flexible but it is not necessary for a charity shop manager to have a 'good sense of humour', neither can such a quality be objectively defined.

**tip**

Adapt job descriptions and person specifications from those developed for similar jobs in other organisations. It may be possible to ask other organisations for copies of the relevant documents, or request job descriptions and person specifications for similar posts advertised in the press.

## Setting salary levels and hours

It is important to get salary levels and the hours of work right. Salary is one of the key factors that applicants consider when looking for a job. As well as the fundamental question of whether the job pays enough to cover living expenses, salary also indicates the level of the job and whether it is a realistic prospect for the applicant. It is unlikely that someone on a current salary of £20,000 would apply for a £50,000 job, but it would not be over ambitious to apply for a post paying £25,000. Salaries should be appropriate to the relative seniority of the post, the responsibility of the role and the required skills and experience of the postholder. Where there are existing staff within an organisation, there should be a proper pay structure which will include any new posts. The contracted hours

---

**VOLUNTARY SECTOR MYTHS**

*Myth:* 'People work in the sector because they are committed to the cause. We don't have to pay them much.'

*Reality:* It is true that voluntary sector pay is generally less than comparable posts in the corporate sector and that voluntary sector staff largely accept this, perhaps because they are committed to the cause, because the work is more flexible, or because organisational structures are less hierarchical. Whatever the reason, this does not justify deliberate underpayment. Although it may save money in the short term, this approach is counter-productive as it will discourage many suitable candidates from applying for the post and staff will feel exploited and undervalued, often resulting in high staff turnover. It also undermines equal opportunities, as only those staff who can afford to be poorly paid, usually because they have another source of income, will take the jobs. This is particularly a problem in areas of high employment and housing costs.

*Myth:* 'Part-time staff always put in extra hours, so why pay for a full time worker?'

*Reality:* It is true that many part-time staff do work additional hours when necessary but this should not be a weekly occurrence due to the demands of the workload. People chose to work part-time because of their domestic commitments or other lifestyle choices and many will not be prepared or able to work unpaid hours. To pay someone to work part time and expect him or her to put in a 35-hour week is exploitative.

should be realistic for the amount of work involved, and this should be checked by calculating the volume of work involved per week for each of the tasks within the job description. Poor pay and part-time posts are not uncommon in the voluntary sector, but there are myths regarding both (see box on p. 98 above).

Charities adopt a variety of approaches for determining salaries.

1  Many local charities base staff salaries on local authority pay scales, for example setting the remuneration of a project worker at the same level as a social worker and a project manager at the level of a senior social worker or social work manager.

2  Another option is to gather information about the salaries of comparable workers in other organisations. Look for posts with a similar level of responsibility and requiring similar skills and experience. This could be done either by contacting organisations directly or through reviewing job adverts in the papers.

3  Where the organisation has a pay structure in place, consider the responsibilities of the post and the position within the organisational hierarchy when setting pay levels.

4  Consider regional variations – accommodation and transport costs are generally much higher in London and the South East and this is reflected in salaries and salary expectations.

**CAUTION!**

When considering the amount your charity can afford to pay in salary, remember to include employers' national insurance contributions. This is the amount employers are required to pay in national insurance in respect of each member of staff. Contributions are calculated as a percentage of any salary above the earnings threshold. Rates and the threshold are subject to change every April, but as a rough guide contributions have recently been around 12–13% of salary above £4,500.

The Inland Revenue publishes information on the current rates (www.inlandrevenue.gov.uk/rates/nic.htm).

Once job descriptions and person specifications are in place and salaries and hours of work have been set, it is time to start the recruitment process.

## The recruitment process

### Where to advertise?

Recruitment advertising is expensive but worthwhile as it is in the charity's interest for information about the post to be available to as many people as possible. Many charities try to save resources by recruiting through word of mouth and a selection of newsletters. However, this restricts the people who are informed of the vacancy to those who are in the charity's communication loop. As a result, equal opportunities practice is undermined and potential candidates may be overlooked. Instead, it is best practice to advertise in publicly available media, including general newspapers and specialist press. The internet now provides another advertising opportunity.

The choice of advertising media will depend on the nature of the job and the person specification, with the location of the advert targeted at the most likely applicants. People looking for jobs will review the publications that best suit their requirements, so consider whether jobs should be advertised nationally or locally, in the general press, in sector specific media or in publications targeted at professionals. As a rule of thumb, national jobs should be nationally advertised. Within this, trustees may decide to target the voluntary sector itself, for example through Wednesday's *Guardian* or trade publications such as *Third Sector*. Alternatively, trustees may decide to target a particular profession, for example through the IT pages of national newspapers or through professional journals such as *Community Care* (a weekly publication on social work issues). This latter approach will be particularly relevant if the person specification requires an identified qualification (in this case in social work) as an essential requirement but will be less suitable if this is only one of the acceptable qualifications specified alongside, say, a youth work or teaching qualification.

There may also be occasions when it is appropriate to advertise through lifestyle publications or those targeted at minority groups; for example, when recruiting staff to work within the gay and lesbian community or particular ethnic groups.

Just because national jobs should be advertised nationally, this does not mean local jobs should only be advertised locally. Trustees should consider the nature of the job, the rate of pay, the skills required and whether people would be prepared to travel to work or relocate to take up the post. Local newspapers, even when part of a group of publications, tend to have limited geographic circulation and their recruitment advertising pages tend to focus on semi-skilled and unskilled jobs. Local advertising may, therefore, be entirely appropriate for care workers or administrative assistants, but not for managers or development workers.

**tip**

> Draw up a list of possible publications and websites for your recruitment advertisement. Review the recruitment pages to see whether they include posts similar to the vacancy you will be advertising. Telephone some of the organisations which have placed adverts and ask them what volume of response (and the quality of the responses) they have had to their advertisement.

Many voluntary sector funders will include recruitment costs for new workers within the amount of any grant. When replacing existing staff, there is often a delay between the departure of the previous employee and the start date of the new employee. This salary underspend can be used to finance recruitment advertisements. A rough guide would be to spend up to one month's salary on the advertising fee.

### What to say?

Recruitment advertisements need to catch the eye of potential applicants, but they also need to communicate enough information to enable people to decide whether they want to request further details. As a minimum they should state:

- the name of the employer;
- the title of the post;
- the salary;
- the hours of work (including any evening or weekend work);
- the place of work;
- the key elements of the job;
- the skills and experience required of applicants, including any definite restrictions or requirements, e.g. any professional qualification required;
- the deadline for applications;
- the date of interviews (often expressed as a week, rather than a specific day); and

- how to obtain further information. If a 24-hour answerphone is available, this should be stated on the advert.

Many adverts also contain a statement regarding the charity's commitment to equal opportunities.

Job adverts may quote salary as a range, e.g. £22,000–£25,000 depending on the experience of the worker or as a starting salary with progression to the upper level. If the post is part time, the advert should clearly state whether the salary quoted is for those hours or work, e.g. '£12,571 for 20 hours', or whether it is the full-time salary which will be reduced to take account of the part-time hours, e.g. '£22,000 pro rata.'

In describing the main aspects of the role, organisations often include the challenges as well as the positive elements of the job.

## Application packs or CVs?

It is good equal opportunities practice to use application packs and forms rather than to request CVs. This ensures that the same information is asked of all applicants and that applicants can specifically describe the relevance of their skills and experience to the advertised post. Applicants can, of course, attach their CVs if they wish.

Application packs should contain information about the organisation and the post. As a minimum they should contain the job description, person specification and application form. Many organisations also include documents such as the latest annual report, publicity literature and information about the background or context of the post. It is good practice to keep a record of the application packs distributed.

Application forms should request the following information:
- name and contact details;
- qualifications;
- work history, i.e. previous employers, job titles and responsibilities;
- other relevant experience, e.g. voluntary work and personal interests;
- supporting information: here applicants should be invited to explain how they meet the person specification;
- references;
- equal opportunities monitoring form. The monitoring form should be separate from or detachable from the main application form. The monitoring form should not include any data that identifies the applicant but should ask for information on ethnicity, gender and

disability. Once received, these forms should be separated from the application and used by the organisation to monitor the number of applications received from minority groups.

For many charities, the cost and time involved in sending acknowledgements to every applicant is prohibitive. If this is the case, include in the application pack a statement to the effect that only shortlisted applicants will be contacted, or ask applicants to enclose a stamped addressed envelope or postcard that will be returned to them as receipt of their application.

## Shortlisting, interviews and making your decision

Before shortlisting applicants for interview, the organisation should agree who will be on the interviewing panel. For senior positions, the panel should include at least one trustee. The interview panel should be involved in the shortlisting process, with additional input from other trustees or staff members as appropriate. It is important for the person who will be managing the new staff member to be involved at this stage.

Shortlisting should be based solely on the information submitted in the application and should focus on the extent to which each candidate meets the requirements of the person specification. Those who meet the requirements most closely should be invited for interview. The ideal number of candidates to interview is between four and six. This provides adequate numbers for comparison whilst remaining manageable.

The purpose of the interview is to gain additional information about the candidates and assess their suitability for the job and the organisation. The interviews should be planned in advance and all questions and tests should be relevant to the post. For example, a project manager may be required to give presentations in the course of the job, so it would be reasonable to ask candidates to give a presentation as part of the interview. However, the same would not be true of an administrative assistant, although applicants for that post could fairly be required to undertake a typing test. Under good equal opportunities practice, every candidate should have the same interview experience. This means that all candidates should be asked the same basic questions, although supplementary questions may be asked in relation to information given on the application form or responses during the interview. The interview panel should agree the questions in advance, the information they hope to receive in response ('model answers'), who will ask each question, and how the responses will be scored.

Interview questions should address applicants' previous experience and its relevance to the post, their skills in the context of the job (e.g. do they have the necessary analytical skills to summarise consultation papers and debate the key issues arising from them?) and their ability to deal with any challenges inherent to the job or the organisation. Scenario questions can be very useful, i.e. 'what would you do if ...?'. Interview panels should not be wary of addressing any difficult issues relating to the post. If the role involves working with challenging individuals, ask applicants what experience they have had of similar situations and how they have managed them.

The scoring methods used in interviews vary in terms of the totals used (e.g. marks out of 3, 5 or 6) and whether the interview panel debate and agree a score against each question or simply add all the scores of individual panel members together. Similarly, some questions may be considered more important than others and the scores weighted accordingly. The approach to scoring should be consistent across all candidates, and the model answers agreed by the interview panel can be extremely helpful here. When scoring responses, interviewers should remember that few applicants will be able to answer every question perfectly, but it is important to find someone with the potential to do the job. In this context relevant skills and a willingness and ability to learn can be more valuable than knowledge.

Scoring is useful in bringing objectivity into the assessment of candidates, but is rarely adequate on its own. Although interview panels should not be unduly swayed by a candidate's personality, this can have a significant bearing on an individual's ability to work within the organisation. What impact would an introvert chief executive have on an extrovert staff team or vice versa? Would the candidate be accepted by the client group? Less formal selection procedures can be used to help make these decisions: for example, all candidates could be invited to lunch with the staff team or a group of users. Staff and users could then be invited to give their feedback on the applicants to the interview panel. This 'trial by sandwich' interview is frequently used in the voluntary sector.

Second interviews, with a slightly different panel, may be appropriate for senior jobs or appointments where the interview panel is having difficulty deciding between two or more candidates.

The favoured candidate should be offered the position subject to references. If he or she refuses the position, the interview panel will need to consider whether any of the other candidates interviewed were suitable or whether the post should be re-advertised. Unsuccessful candidates should be offered feedback.

The time it takes to appoint new staff can be surprisingly lengthy, as illustrated in the table below.

The timescale shows the recruitment process from the placement of the advert, assuming that job descriptions etc. are already in place. In reality the process may take much longer. Where an existing member of staff is being replaced, it is good practice to review the job description and person specification before recruitment starts. This, together with agreeing the wording of the advert, can easily add another couple of weeks to the process.

Consider this timescale when determining the notice periods of your staff. If the charity really cannot function with a particular post being vacant, it may be useful to set a longer notice period than the standard one month, so that the length of vacancy is eliminated or at least minimised. Unfortunately this is of little benefit if the appointee also has a long notice period in his or her current role.

---

### TIMESCALE FOR RECRUITMENT AND SELECTION

*Week 1:* Place advertisement. Allow at least three weeks for applicants to request and receive application packs and then complete and return them.

*Week 4:* Shortlisting by interview panel and invitations to interview. Allow at least one week for shortlisting and sending out invitations and a minimum of one week's notice for shortlisted candidates.

*Week 6:* Interviews and offer. Allow a week for interview, decision, offer and acceptance. Many candidates will not resign from their current post until they have received a written offer. Further time will be required for taking up references. Although telephone references are quick, they should always be followed up in writing.

Once an offer has been accepted and satisfactory references provided, the new employee can start work, subject to the notice period of his or her existing job if currently employed. This could be up to three months or even longer for senior posts.

Total: 11 weeks +

---

When the successful candidate accepts the post, references should be taken up and start dates agreed. Other practical issues such as arranging desk space and computer log-ins and setting up payroll, etc will also need to be considered. Organisations with a sizeable staff team may have internal structures in place for paying staff, deducting PAYE tax and national insurance and paying employers' national insurance contributions. Smaller organisations may buy in payroll services from other agencies. This service is often provided at low or no cost to local charities by local authorities (especially where the local authority is the funder), councils for voluntary services and community accountancy schemes.

### When to use an agency

Rather than manage the whole recruitment and selection process themselves, some charities chose to use a recruitment agency. Agencies cater for every level of recruitment with some being sector or job specific, so whether recruiting for a care worker or chief executive, there will be an appropriate agency.

The input of agencies into the process varies, with some drawing solely from their client base and others placing adverts. The agency may shortlist a number of possible candidates from its existing clients and pass these forward for interview. Alternatively, it may actively solicit applications for the post, conduct initial interviews and pass a few candidates to the charity for final selection.

The charges made by agencies for these services vary, often taking the form of a percentage of salary for a successful placement. It can be an expensive form of recruitment, placing it beyond the reach of many charities, but it can be valuable to organisations that do not have the time, the skills or the contacts to manage the process themselves.

## Defining boundaries

One of the most difficult problems within charities, and one that frequently leads to friction, is drawing a line between the work of staff and trustees. As has been seen in the earlier chapters of this book, trustees have wide-ranging responsibilities and these responsibilities cannot be delegated. It is the trustees who are ultimately responsible, and liable, for the charity. However, trustees can delegate tasks that need to be conducted in the execution of their responsibilities. We have also seen that, in individual charities, trustees often take on roles that extend way beyond their legal responsibilities, for example by becoming involved in the operation of the charity. It is in the area of these delegated tasks and additional trustee activities that boundaries often become blurred.

The importance of agreeing the boundaries between trustee and staff activities can not be overemphasised. Where boundaries are ill defined, there is a risk of staff and trustees tripping over each other in attempting to do the same work, leading at best to an unnecessary duplication of effort and at worst to resentment, mixed messages and the appearance of managerial incompetence. At the other extreme, whole aspects of activity risk being lost in a no man's land between trustee and staff roles.

So how can this be avoided? Unfortunately there is no model solution. The distinctions between trustee and staff workloads will vary between organisations and within organisations over time. A useful starting point is for trustees to identify those areas of their responsibility over which they want to retain complete control and those where they are prepared to delegate tasks to employees. This was discussed earlier in the chapter when we looked at the function of staff and drafting job descriptions. In this context the value of the job description is apparent, as it provides documentary evidence of the boundaries. This can be further supported by including discussion of boundaries within the induction programme for new staff and trustees. Similarly, the business plan and other planning tools can be used to determine the work plans of both staff and trustees.

Circumstances will, however, inevitably arise which fall outside anybody's job description or work plan and both trustees and staff will often need to be flexible in determining responsibility for areas that are beyond the usual parameters. In order for such dilemmas to be negotiated appropriately, it is crucial that there is mutual respect between the trustees and the staff. This means that staff must acknowledge the overarching responsibilities of trustees and their need to retain control, whilst trustees must respect the fact that staff are paid to do a job and have been appointed, hopefully, because they have the skills and experience necessary to do the job properly. In this sense, you must allow your staff to get on with the job that they are paid to do.

Any problems that do arise should be discussed through appropriate procedures, i.e. line management, supervision and appraisal. The usual management structure in charities is for the most senior employee to report to the chair of the board of trustees, and for that employee to then manage any other staff. In large organisations there may be several layers of staff management. Some charities, particularly those with fairly flat internal management structures, operate a system where the various members of the senior staff are each managed by different trustees. Although there is a degree of common sense in this approach in that workloads are shared, its success rests on strong communication between the trustees. Without good communication it is unlikely that the trustees will give consistent messages to the staff team.

Particular problems may arise where trustees also act as volunteers for the organisation and are then co-ordinated or managed by staff who are employed to run the service. This can be an awkward situation for staff and trustees alike and, again, there needs to be a mutual respect as to each other's roles. The trustees in question need to recognise that the worker

---

**CASE EXAMPLE**

A charity providing domiciliary services to people with disabilities had a staff team of 15 people. The majority of employees were care workers, with the senior employee responsible for management of the service and administrative duties. Trustees set policy in relation to quality standards for the service provided and health and safety issues. One of the care workers contacted the senior employee with concerns regarding the administration of medicines. The senior employee directed the worker as to the appropriate course of action and communicated the information to the other care workers so that they would know what to do in similar circumstances.

The trustees felt that the senior employee had acted outside her authority by instructing the worker on a health and safety issue. However the employee believed that her actions were justified as it was a management issue and the advice she had given was consistent with organisational policy, as determined by the trustees. The incident was discussed in a regular line management meeting between the senior employee and the chair, with both sides presenting their arguments. The senior employee explained that the situation had required a swift response and she had acted within the terms of the health and safety policy and the organisation's insurance. She also highlighted her staff management role and her nursing background, believing that this qualified her to make such decisions. The chair accepted this argument.

---

**CASE EXAMPLE**

A small charity had been running a day centre for older people for some years. The service had been run on an entirely voluntary basis, but this was becoming harder to sustain and the trustees sought and gained funding to appoint a manager.

The post was advertised and the job description and person specification clearly stated that the role would include management responsibilities, and this was also reflected in the salary. An appropriately skilled professional was appointed. When he started work the trustees handed over administrative and operational tasks, but continued to act as volunteers, attending the centre on a daily basis and giving instructions to the other volunteers. The manager's role was regularly undermined by the trustees and he resigned within six months.

---

has been appointed to manage the service and must be empowered to do so. The trustees should value the experience and opinions of the worker just as the worker should recognise that trustees with an understanding of operational practice and the issues faced by users are valuable board members. The situation may be helped by clear guidance to all volunteers of their role in operational issues and the responsibility of the employees to ensure the quality and safety of the service.

## The chair/chief executive relationship

As has been mentioned earlier in this chapter, it is usually the chair of the board of trustees who manages the most senior employee. The term 'chief executive' is commonly used in the voluntary sector and is used here to describe the most senior staff role, whatever the actual title used.

It is not overstating the case to say that the success, or otherwise, of a charity frequently rests on the quality of this relationship. A positive, strong working relationship between chair and chief executive can lead a charity to great successes. At the other extreme, a poor relationship can cripple the organisation. Poor relationships take a variety of forms:

- *Strong chair/strong chief executive.* This blend can be an asset to the charity, if the chair and chief executive work in harmony; however, if they do not, the resulting conflict will stifle any development and undermine the morale of the organisation as a whole.

- *Strong chair/weak chief executive.* In this circumstance, the chief executive may not be empowered to do his or her job and may end up working within a very small comfort zone. This is clearly unhealthy for organisational progress.
- *Weak chair/strong chief executive.* This relationship can undermine the authority of the governing body as there is a strong risk that the chief executive will manage the board, rather than the other way round. Although this may seem like an advantageous situation for chief executives, they will have little direction or constructive feedback from the board and will find themselves stranded when they most need support.
- *Weak chair/weak chief executive.* Charities that suffer from this governance/management relationship are likely to stagnate.

The ideal chair/chief executive relationship is an elusive balance between the two roles, where both are equipped to carry out their roles competently and with vision but without conflict. Chairs should lead the board in setting the direction of the charity and chief executives should act as the bridge between policy and operation, board and staff, in their turn leading the staff team in reaching the charity's destination.

The relationship between chair and chief executive is so crucial that charities should invest time and resources in cultivating it, starting at the recruitment stage. Chairs and chief executives should discuss their relative roles and working relationship. Where conflicts cannot be resolved by internal means, it may be worth calling on the support of an independent mediator.

## The role of staff in supporting trustees

As the governing body of the organisation, one of the trustees' functions is to provide staff with the resources and support they need to achieve their job description. However the relationship works both ways. Staff also have a role in supporting the trustees in executing their responsibilities and some staff may be appointed expressly for this purpose.

By virtue of their daily involvement, staff have an in-depth working knowledge of their organisation that is rarely experienced by voluntary trustees. They also have a range of professional skills and support networks that are not present or otherwise available to the trustee board. Similarly, staff may have time available and access to technology that may not be available to the trustees. As a result, staff often play a key role in supporting the board.

This support may take a variety of forms, ranging from agenda planning and minute taking, induction of trustees (see chapter 3), arranging trustee training and providing speeches or briefings, through to providing the trustees with the information necessary for the board to make decisions regarding the charity. Such information or training may be general or specific to the charity. For example, staff are often responsible for passing information to trustees on wider legal issues, but will also play a key role in informing trustees about the charity's services and finances and opportunities for development. It is not uncommon in well-staffed charities for senior staff to present complex reports to trustees, analysing wide-ranging information regarding the charity and the wider context of its operation and considering the different options for action and the implications of each. Whilst trustees should value this support (it is, after all, what the charity pays its staff for) they should not lose overall control, for no matter how competent the staff, it is the trustees who retain responsibility and liability for the charity.

Staff should also be wary of stepping outside the boundaries of their employment contracts. This is particularly true for staff of charitable companies as the concept of 'shadow directors' means that staff (or other non-board members) who have directed the board may share the responsibility and liability of the board for the decisions made.

## Role of the company secretary

Charities with a company secretary (a legal requirement for registered companies) have the benefit of an appointment that is dedicated to supporting the governance of the organisation. Whether the company secretary is a post in its own right or whether the role is combined with that of the chief executive, finance director, other senior staff member, or a trustee, it is the company secretary's responsibility to ensure that the charity is run within the law and according to the terms of its governing document. A key element of this role is to support the trustees in navigating their way through legal and constitutional requirements. This includes ensuring that trustees are correctly appointed and inducted and that board and members' meetings are properly run. In fulfilling this role, company secretaries work extremely closely with the board, particularly the chair.

Smaller companies may fall into the trap of appointing a company secretary because this is a legal requirement, without giving due attention to the demands of the role. Signing annual returns is only a minor element of the company secretarial function but demonstrates the significant responsibility that the secretary has for the probity of the organisation. Company secretaries in charities should have a sound knowledge of both company and charity law and a basic knowledge of other legislation affecting the organisation and should use this knowledge in supporting and advising the trustees. In particular, they should identify danger zones and advise trustees to call on appropriate professional advice when necessary.

The interpretation of the company secretary's function will vary from one organisation to another, but company secretaries' activities often include responsibility for property and insurance issues, internal controls and audits and provision of information to regulators. They may also take responsibility for ensuring legal compliance in areas such a fundraising and employment.

---

**PROPOSED CHANGES – THE COMPANY SECRETARY**

The law requiring the appointment of a company secretary in all registered companies is likely to change as a result of the government's review of company law. The Government has issued a White Paper which reflects its intention to abolish the requirement for private companies to appoint a company secretary, meaning that charitable companies limited by guarantee would not be required to have a company secretary, although they might chose to do so.

Trustees of charitable companies are advised to keep an eye on developments.

---

## Resolving conflicts

As soon as an organisation employs staff, it should develop appropriate procedures for resolving conflict within the staff team and between staff and trustees. It is also good practice to have policies in place relating to conflicts involving volunteers.

Conflicts come in many forms. An occasional difference of opinion between individuals is normal and is often swiftly resolved by those directly involved. Where such differences continue and have an impact on the operation of the organisation, for example because of deteriorating internal communications, it may still be possible to address the conflict through informal means, for example if a manager or other third party is able to mediate in the dispute. There will, however be circumstances that require a more structured response. These may be disciplinary issues, i.e. a member of staff has acted outside the terms of employment or his or her conduct is unacceptable, or they may be grievances by staff against another person within the organisation. Written procedures should be developed to deal with both scenarios.

It can be useful to establish disciplinary and grievance procedures in partnership or consultation with the staff. Employees will most likely have strong opinions on what is, and is not, acceptable behaviour and an open approach to policy development encourages joint ownership of and commitment to the policy. It may also be appropriate to consider extending the policy to include volunteers. For trustees, sitting at the top of the organisation, the disciplinary procedure will be invoked to deal with serious staff management problems, whereas the grievance procedure may be used within the staff team, by staff against trustees, or by trustees against each other.

The disciplinary and grievance procedures are sometimes combined, as they are often jointly invoked, for example by a manager disciplining a member of staff whilst that employee launches a grievance against the manager. Procedures have a number of key features, such as:

- the scope of the procedure (i.e. the definition of the people and circumstances covered by it);
- the norms of accepted behaviours: these may be related to professional standards and/or organisational culture and are sometimes presented as a separate code of conduct;
- the means of invoking the procedure, such as to whom the grievance or disciplinary concern should be reported and how;
- the different levels of the procedure, such as informal complaint, formal complaint and a means of moving through the levels;
- the different sanctions under the procedure, such as written warnings, the length of time warnings stay on personnel files, suspension and dismissal;
- the relationship between the different sanctions, e.g. three written warnings lead to dismissal;
- a description of gross misconduct, leading to summary dismissal;

- treatment of criminal convictions and misconduct outside the workplace;
- means of dealing with unfounded or mischievous grievances;
- the process for dealing with a joint disciplinary and grievance complaint;
- the approach to collective grievances (this may depend on whether it is an industrial relations type grievance, such as pay and conditions, or a personnel issue, e.g. bullying by a manager);
- the process for handling public interest concerns (whistleblowing);
- rights of representation to those using the procedures: there may be a right to bring a friend or advocate to meetings;
- description of those who will be responsible for handling the complaint (including the efforts that will be made to avoid one person being responsible for both making the allegation and taking the decision, and provisions for taking the matter outside of normal line management arrangements, e.g. in sensitive cases);
- any appeals procedure; and
- a disclaimer regarding the completeness of the policy and its extension to unanticipated events.

Charities may also choose to include statements relating to certain disciplinary or grievance issues: for example, racist or sexist behaviour, bullying, harassment and health and safety risks.

---

**SAMPLE DISCIPLINARY/GRIEVANCE PROCEDURE**

1   The organisation seeks to maintain a safe and productive working environment for all staff, trustees and volunteers, free from discrimination, harassment and intimidation.

2   The organisation recognises that there may be cases where individuals become concerned about the conduct of those working in the organisation and places a responsibility on all parties to attempt to resolve such issues in the first instance without recourse to this procedure. In particular, concerns about staff performance or misconduct should be dealt with as part of the normal line management process.

3   This procedure shall be invoked in the following circumstances:
- where problems have not been successfully resolved by informal means;

*cont.*

## SAMPLE DISCIPLINARY/GRIEVANCE PROCEDURE  continued

- repeated cases of minor misconduct or minor grievances; and
- serious misconduct or grievances, particularly in relation to discrimination, harassment, breaches of confidentiality, health and safety risks, criminal conduct and other public interest concerns.

4  All concerns falling under paragraph 3 must be reported to the Chief Executive. The Chief Executive will be responsible for determining whether to invoke the formal procedure.

### Formal process

5  The Chief Executive will be responsible for all action under the formal process, except where he/she has been implicated in the disciplinary concern or grievance, in which case the chair of the board's staffing sub-committee will be responsible.

6  Issues that could result in the dismissal of a member of staff will be subject to a final hearing by the staffing sub-committee.

7  Upon instigating the formal disciplinary/grievance procedure, all parties to the concern will be informed in writing of the allegations or grievance raised, the steps that will be taken for the investigation and the timescale set for completion of the process.

8  Grievances will be addressed, in the first instance, by an informal arbitration hearing led by the Chief Executive or chair of the staffing sub-committee (if the Chief Executive is implicated in the grievance) and attended by the parties to the grievance. If the employee is not satisfied with the outcome of the arbitration hearing, he/she may request that the grievance progress to formal hearing. Such a request must be made within five working days of the arbitration hearing.

9  If it is discovered beyond all reasonable doubt, at any point during the consideration of a disciplinary concern or grievance, that the allegations are unfounded then the procedure will be immediately halted. Staff who are believed to have deliberately or maliciously raised unfounded or inaccurate allegations may be subject to disciplinary action.

10  All disciplinary concerns that are subject to this procedure will be decided by a formal hearing.

11  All employees have a right to be represented or supported at formal hearings by a colleague, trade union official, friend or

*cont.*

**SAMPLE DISCIPLINARY/GRIEVANCE PROCEDURE continued**

other advocate and have the right to reasonable paid time off to prepare evidence for the hearing.

12 The organisation may call on the advice of external bodies as appropriate.

13 Full details of the complaint, evidence and witnesses should be communicated in writing to the affected employee at least five working days before the formal hearing.

14 The employee must provide, in writing, details of any evidence or witnesses that will be called upon to refute the allegations, no later than 24 hours before the time of the formal hearing.

15 At the hearing, the Chief Executive will present the complaint and any evidence supporting the complaint. The affected employee and/or representative may then present the defence and any supporting evidence.

16 The decision will be made by the Chief Executive, with reference to the staffing sub-committee and/or external advisers as appropriate. Decisions will be made on the balance of probability.

17 The decision will be communicated to the employee and the individual who initiated the process. If the misconduct allegation is not proven or the grievance not justified, no further action will be taken and reference to the complaint will be removed from employment records three months after the conclusion of the hearing. If the case is proven, the employee may make a statement in mitigation.

### Sanctions

18 Sanctions (and the length of time that they remain on employees' records) will depend on the severity and frequency of the complaint:
- First written warning (for first and minor offences): one year
- Further written warning (for repeated or continuing concerns): two years
- Final written warning (the last step before dismissal): indefinitely
- Dismissal with notice (for repeated problems that have not been resolved)
- Summary dismissal (for cases of gross misconduct without mitigating circumstances)

19 The process is intended to be cumulative; however, there may be instances where the severity of the incident warrants a higher sanction than would be implemented under the cumulative approach.

*cont.*

## SAMPLE DISCIPLINARY/GRIEVANCE PROCEDURE  continued

### Gross misconduct

20  Where gross misconduct is alleged, the employee in question will be suspended on full pay pending the decision at formal hearing. During the suspension period the employee may only enter the premises by arrangement with the Chief Executive for the purposes of gathering evidence to defend the allegation.

### Appeals

21  Employees may appeal against decisions made and sanctions imposed under this procedure. Appeals must be presented in writing within one calendar month of the original decision. Appeals will be heard by the staffing sub-committee in respect of decisions made by the Chief Executive and by the full trustee board in respect of decisions made by the staffing sub-committee or its chair.

22  Appeals will be subject to the same process as the original hearing but may only consider those factors in dispute.

23  The appeal body may overrule or uphold the decision of the original hearing and impose any of the available sanctions.

### Joint grievance/disciplinary issues

24  Where a grievance has been raised in response to or resulted in a disciplinary allegation, the disciplinary matter will be dealt with first. The employee raising the grievance will be entitled to present the grievance as part of the disciplinary process. If any elements of the grievance remain unresolved at the conclusion of the disciplinary process, these may be addressed separately within this procedure.

### Collective grievances

25  Employee concerns about pay and conditions and statutory provisions outside of the control of the organisation should be raised through staff meetings rather than the grievance procedure.

26  Collective grievances may be raised in response to concerns about the conduct of a member of staff, volunteer or trustee.

### Whistleblowing

27  The organisation encourages staff to disclose information where they believe that the safety of employees, volunteers, trustees, clients or the general public is at risk or the probity of
*cont.*

**117**

## SAMPLE DISCIPLINARY/GRIEVANCE PROCEDURE continued

the organisation is being undermined. Such concerns should be initially raised through the grievance procedure. Individuals should only report such concerns to external bodies if all stages of this procedure have been implemented without successful resolution, there is an immediate risk to public safety or a crime has been, or is likely to be, committed.

28 Individuals who raise genuine grievances where wider disclosure is in the public interest will not be subject to prejudicial treatment from or within the organisation.

### Timescales

29 Arbitration hearings will be held within 10 working days of a grievance being formally raised.

30 Formal disciplinary hearings will take place within 20 working days of the procedure being invoked.

31 If compliance with these timescales is not possible, the Chief Executive will provide all parties to the hearing with a revised timescale and reasons for the delay.

### Appendix – Definitions of misconduct

The following examples are indicative of the behaviour that is considered to represent misconduct and do not represent a comprehensive list. Behaviour may move between the gross misconduct and misconduct categories, depending on circumstances.

### Gross misconduct

Theft, deceit, dishonesty
Violence
Wilful damage to property
Harassment
Sexual misconduct
Discrimination
Breaches of client confidentiality
Refusal to carry out reasonable
   instructions
Criminal offences directly related to
   the employee's work or bringing
   the charity into disrepute

### Misconduct

Deliberate poor performance
Abuse of employment rights and
   privileges
Failure to carry out reasonable
   instructions
Failure to comply with policy and
   procedures
Disruptive behaviour
Absenteeism and poor time keeping

Organisations with 20 or more staff are required to have a disciplinary procedure and it is good practice for smaller organisations to follow this example. As can be seen, the disciplinary and grievance procedure is essential for resolving staff management issues and is crucial in terms of employment law. If staff are dismissed unfairly or feel forced to resign due to the conduct of their colleagues or employers, the trustees may be called before an employment tribunal to justify their actions and may be required to pay compensation. A strong procedure correctly implemented may be the best defence available to trustees.

---

**PROPOSED CHANGES – DISCIPLINARY AND GRIEVANCE PROCEDURES**

The Employment Act 2002 provides standard disciplinary and grievance procedures. When this is brought into force, these will be implied into contracts of employment.

---

## Whistleblowing

The law protects employees who report concerns about misconduct or malpractice in their employer when to do so is in the public interest. The protection is limited to the right not to suffer any detriment because of the disclosure. This includes dismissal, dismissal in the guise of redundancy, victimisation and demotion. In order to enjoy legal protection, such disclosures must be made in good faith and the reasonable belief that the information reveals that one of the following has happened, is happening, or is likely to happen:

- a criminal offence;
- failure to comply with a legal obligation (statutory or contractual);
- endangerment of health and safety;
- environmental damage; or
- concealment of information.

In addition, the disclosure must be made either to: the employer (or a person nominated by the employer in internal procedures); the person whose actions are in question; a legal adviser in the course of obtaining advice; or a person or body prescribed by the Secretary of State.

Employees who bypass internal disclosure and go straight to an external body will be protected provided that, in addition to the above, the disclosure has not been made for personal gain, it is reasonable for the disclosure to be made and either:

1   the employee reasonably believes that he or she will be victimised by disclosing to the employer;
2   the employee has already made the disclosure internally; or
3   there is no prescribed body for disclosure to be made to and the employee believes that disclosure to the employer will result in the destruction or concealment of evidence.

Normal channels may also be bypassed in exceptionally serious cases that may be more appropriately reported to a third party, such as the police.

It is advisable to include whistleblowing within any disciplinary/grievance procedure or other internal policies.

## Legal issues

Recent years have seen extensive legislative changes in relation to employment issues. The following section gives an overview of the requirements; however the law can be complex and all organisations employing paid staff are advised to seek appropriate legal advice regarding their individual responsibilities.

### Employment contracts

The contractual relationship between employer and employee is determined by a combination of written documents and conduct. However in the interests of clarity it is good practice to provide employees with a written contract describing their terms and conditions of service. As a legal minimum, employers must provide all staff who are employed for longer than one month with a written 'statement of particulars' describing the key terms and conditions of employment. This should be issued to staff within two months of starting work and should contain the following:

- identity of employer;
- identity of employee;
- job title;
- start date (if the employee has changed jobs within the organisation, the original employment date should also be included);

- normal place of work (for home-based or travelling workers, include the base to which they report or the head office);
- remuneration, which should be a scale rather than specific figure (this allows you to increase salary by letter, rather than revising the statement of particulars) and should include non-salary elements of the package;
- working hours;
- period of employment (if fixed or temporary);
- holiday entitlement;
- maternity etc. leave entitlements;
- notice period;
- sick pay entitlement;
- pension provision and retirement age;
- disciplinary and grievance arrangements;
- trade union recognition and other arrangements for collective agreements; and
- signatures.

Issues such as maternity leave entitlement, pension provision and any disciplinary/grievance procedure are likely to be covered by detailed documents. It is acceptable for the statement of particulars to make reference to these documents and how they can be obtained (e.g. in the staff handbook or on the organisation's intranet site) rather than to include the full text within the statement.

It is worth including information on any probation period in the statement of particulars, especially if different terms and conditions apply during this time (e.g. shorter notice periods).

## Equal pay and anti-discrimination

Employees have the right to equal pay for work of equal value. This applies to the overall package (not just salary) and includes other non-pay conditions such as working hours. In addition, all employees have a right not to be discriminated against on the grounds of gender, race or marital status. Rules against discrimination on the grounds of disability only apply to organisations employing 15 or more staff (although this limit may be abolished in the future). The law relates to both the selection and ongoing employment of staff and covers both direct and indirect discrimination and victimisation.

## Sick pay and leave

The majority of employees are entitled to Statutory Sick Pay (SSP) provided they supply a self-certificate explaining the reasons for the first week of absence and doctors' certificates for any subsequent absence. Trustees may, and many do, provide for more generous terms as part of the contract of employment. Often this involves a set period of sickness absence on full pay followed by a similar period on half pay. In determining your policy on sick pay, consider what length of absence and rate of pay the charity can afford, both in terms of finances and operational impact, and balance this against the charity's values as a supportive employer.

## Maternity leave

Maternity pay and leave provisions are complex, but the basic arrangements are as follows (for mothers of children born on or after 6 April 2003):

- pregnant women have the right to paid time off for ante-natal care;
- there is a legal minimum of 26 weeks' ordinary maternity leave;
- women who have been employed for at least 26 consecutive weeks at the beginning of the fourteenth week before their estimated week of confinement are entitled to a further 26 weeks' additional maternity leave (giving a maximum total of 52 weeks' maternity leave);
- during the leave period all rights including, e.g. seniority and holiday entitlements, but excluding remuneration, are preserved;
- women have the right to return to the same job or a suitable alternative.

Women who have been continuously employed for 26 weeks up to and including the fifteenth week before their due date and whose income is at or above the National Insurance lower earnings limit are entitled to Statutory Maternity Pay. Those who do not qualify may be able to claim Maternity Allowance, a DSS benefit.

## Adoption leave

The Employment Act 2002 has introduced a right for adoption leave for parents where a child is placed for adoption on or after 6 April 2003. The right is for 26 weeks' ordinary adoption leave, followed by up to 26 weeks' additional adoption leave, giving a maximum of up to 52 weeks' leave. If a couple is adopting jointly, only one parent can take adoption leave but the other parent may be entitled to paternity leave.

## Paternity leave

The father of a child born on or after 6 April 2003 may have a right to a period of either one or two weeks' paid paternity leave within 56 days of the date of birth.

## Family friendly requirements

*Domestic emergency.* Since 1999 employees have had the right to reasonable time off in cases of domestic emergency. This includes caring for a spouse, child, parent or cohabitee, but does not cover lodgers or tenants. The right arises when:

- the dependant is ill, gives birth or is injured or assaulted;
- arrangements need to be made for the care of an ill or injured dependant;
- the dependant dies;
- there is an unexpected disruption of existing care arrangements;
- there is an unexpected incident involving a child at school.

'Reasonable time off' means adequate time to make different arrangements. There is no obligation for the time off to be paid, nor can individuals be obliged to take it as annual leave or time off in lieu of overtime; instead, they may take the time as unpaid leave. Organisations can, of course, make more generous provision for employees, for example by providing for such time off to be paid or extending the availability to include siblings and close friends. Such additional provision should be described within an organisational compassionate leave policy and should be equally available to all staff.

*Parental leave.* The parental leave regulations give both parents the right to thirteen weeks' unpaid leave in respect of children born or adopted after 15 December 1999. Parents must give 21 days' notice of the leave and leave can only be taken in blocks of one week, up to a maximum of four weeks' leave per year. The leave must be taken before the child is five. The provision is extended to the age of 18 in the case of children with disabilities.

Parents have an absolute right to return to the same post unless the leave extends beyond four weeks or is added to maternity leave, in which case employees have the right to return to an appropriate job.

Again, organisations can make more generous provision within their own staff policies.

## Working time regulations

The working time regulations include rights to a working week of a maximum of 48 hours, to regular rest breaks and to four weeks' paid leave. There is a requirement to keep records of working time and these can be inspected by the Health and Safety Executive.

The length of the working week is calculated as an average over a 17-week 'reference period'. This may be extended to 26 weeks and it is possible to agree with the workforce to extend the period to one year. This means that occasional working weeks in excess of 48 hours should not present a problem in law, although they are not good employment practice. Workers may opt out of the 48-hour maximum and autonomous workers who have discretion over their own working hours are not covered, e.g. chief executives.

Workers must have unpaid rest breaks of 20 minutes if they work more than 6 hours, a daily rest of at least 11 hours and a weekly rest of at least 24 hours. Workers may choose not to take these entitlements. Where it is not possible to take these breaks within the working day, 'compensatory rest breaks' should be incorporated into staff rotas.

The right to four weeks' paid leave includes casual workers and there can be no cash substitute except on termination.

Interpreting the application of these regulations within organisations can be extremely complicated, particularly for organisations offering off-site or residential services. Trustees should consider the range of the organisation's work and current staffing arrangements. Trustees should also consider whether it would be acceptable to allow staff to opt out of any of the provisions. The subsequent application of the regulations within the charity should be subject to staff consultation and appropriate legal advice. Arrangements for recording working hours should be compatible with the culture of the charity.

## Part-time workers regulations

Part-time workers have the right not to be treated less favourably than comparable full-time workers. This right applies both to contractual terms and any detriment that may arise due to part time status and extends to job applicants as well as existing employees.

In relation to contractual terms, pay and annual leave should be calculated on a pro rata basis. Employers should also consider entitlement to employee benefits such as pensions and health insurance.

Part-time workers should not be discriminated against in areas such as reorganisation of workload, training and promotion opportunities or redundancy selection. Employers should be cautious in such areas in case they unwittingly discriminate against part-time workers.

## Minimum wage requirements

By law, employers must pay workers at or above the minimum wage. There are two rates of minimum wage, a lower rate for workers aged 18 to 21 and an increased rate for those aged 22 and over. Rates are subject to review, so trustees should check the current rate (see www.inlandrevenue.gov.uk/nmw). As a guide, from 1 October 2002, the lower rate for 18 to 21 year olds was £3.60 and the rate for those aged 22 and over was £4.20.

## Transfer of undertakings

There are complex provisions in place for protecting the terms and conditions of staff where employment is transferred from one organisation to another. In the voluntary sector this may happen, for example, where a charity closes and another charity takes over one of its projects. In such circumstances, staff bring with them the employment conditions (including salary and period of continuous service) that they had with their previous employer prior to the transfer. This can result in complicated arrangements whereby different staff within the organisation operate under different (and potentially incompatible) terms and conditions. Trustees are advised to seek professional guidance before entering such arrangements.

## Trade union recognition

Trade unions have a legal right to gain recognition in the workplace through claiming recognition with an employer. Recognition may take the form of a voluntary agreement between union and employer. Where no such agreement is reached the Central Arbitration Committee (CAC) has a legal right to become involved. If the CAC finds that 50 per cent of the workforce are already trade union members, the CAC will automatically recognise the union. If the figure is less than 50 per cent there must be a ballot. In order for the union to be recognised following a ballot, there must be a majority vote in favour and this must amount to at least 40 per cent of the 'bargaining unit'.

The legislation may have limited impact on smaller charities, but those with large staff teams will be affected. Trustees of larger charities should consider their approach to staff consultation and involvement. For example, consider arrangements for union representation on any staff council, recognition of more than one union within the organisation and how to ensure that the views of staff who are not union members are represented. By taking a proactive approach to canvassing staff opinion, trustees will be better prepared for any subsequent claim for union recognition.

## Stakeholder pensions

Organisations that employ five or more staff are required to make stakeholder pensions available to their employees. Organisations may be exempt from the requirement if they offer an occupational or personal pension scheme to all staff.

Charities must consult with their employees on the selection of the stakeholder provider, although the final decision rests with the charity as employer. A list of providers is available from the Occupational Pensions Regulatory Authority (OPRA).

Trustees should be aware that as employers, they are not liable for the investment performance of the stakeholder pension so employees cannot bring claims against the charity if the pension does not perform well. Trustees should also be aware that, although they can give information to their employees on the pension provision, they can not give advice and to do so could be a criminal offence. This means that trustees must ensure that anybody within the charity who is dealing with queries on stakeholder pensions is aware of the scope and limitations on the information he or she can provide. One solution is to choose a pension provider which can deal directly with staff queries, e.g. through a helpline. In addition, staff contributions are deducted from pay, so the pension provider's administration systems should be compatible with those of the charity.

Employers must make stakeholder pensions available for all staff except:

- those with less than three months' service;
- those with earnings below the National Insurance lower earnings limit;
- those who do not normally live in the UK; and
- those who could have joined an occupational pension scheme offered by the employer but who chose not to do so.

It is up to individual employees to decide whether to take up a stakeholder pension. Pension providers will supply detailed information to help staff make this choice. Employees must complete written applications to join the scheme and specify their level of contribution. Similarly, there is no obligation on employers to make a contribution towards employee pensions, although an employer may decide to do so as a matter of good practice.

## Redundancy

Unfortunately circumstances do arise, often due to lack of funding, where a charity is forced to make some staff redundant. Understandably, the law surrounding redundancies can be complex, and issues such as consultation with staff, redundancy selection, time off for staff to seek new employment and redundancy payments must all be considered. As well as ensuring any redundancy process is technically correct, charity trustees will need to be alert to the potential impact on the charity's reputation and it is advisable to seek professional advice in order to ensure that the process is handled properly and sensitively.

# 7    Accounting, financial management and control

## INTRODUCTION

No matter how worthwhile the work of the charity and no matter how considerable the contribution of volunteers, no organisation can survive in the long term without good financial management and reporting. It is essential for charities to know how much money they have, how much they need and how to manage it wisely, controlling expenditure to ensure that funds are used to further the objects of the charity. Accurate financial information is crucial to the decisions made by the trustees. Trustees cannot sanction the continuation or expansion of the charity's activities without information about the finances available. Similarly, financial indicators may drive any decisions to cut back or cease operations. Financial information, together with the trustees' vision for the direction of the charity, will determine how much the organisation needs to raise, spend and save.

As stated earlier, it is the trustees who are responsible for the charity's financial health and, if they fail in this responsibility, it is the trustees who are personally liable. Trustees also have a responsibility to maximise the income available in order to further the objects of the charity. Therefore it is critical, both from a governance and personal perspective, for trustees to act in full knowledge of the charity's financial situation. This means that all trustees, not just the treasurer, must have or develop the skills to understand the charity's finances and should take an active role in managing those finances in the best interests of the charity. Whilst the treasurer and any staff will play the lead part in financial matters, it is the function of the board as a whole to determine the objectives of financial management and to actively monitor finances.

**CAUTION!**

Charity finance is the subject of many books. It is intended that this chapter will give trustees of small and medium-sized charities a basic understanding of charity finance and demystify some of the terminology used so that trustees can pick up a set of accounts without fear. It is not intended or feasible to cover some of the more technical aspects of charity finance in this guide. Trustees wanting a deeper understanding of charity finance are advised to refer to specialist publications and/or seek professional advice.
Further sources of information are listed in the Directory.

## Charity accounts

Every organisation must produce annual accounts, also known as financial statements. These are vital tools used by trustees and others to monitor the financial status and development of the organisation. Accounts are presented in financial years and each organisation may determine its own financial year. Many charities choose to reflect the national fiscal year by running from 1 April to 31 March, although the calendar year (1 January to 31 December) is also popular.

There are a number of ways of presenting accounts but all have common features:

- name of the organisation and period covered by the accounts (the name should be included as a header on each page);
- income: all accounts must record the amount and sources of income received in the financial year;
- expenditure: accounts must report the expenditure in the financial year, with a breakdown of spending, e.g. staff salaries, accommodation costs, etc.;
- balance sheet: all accounts should include a statement of the charity's funds at the end of the financial year;
- notes to the accounts: these should describe the accounting methods used and give more detailed information on items in the accounts, for example a breakdown of any grants received. They are presented rather like end notes in a book, with numbers given throughout the accounts that identify the corresponding paragraph or table in the notes;
- comparative figures for the previous financial year; and

- signature (with date) of the chair, secretary or treasurer to indicate that the accounts have been accepted and adopted by the board of trustees.

Some organisations are required by law or their governing documents to have their accounts examined by an independent person. In the case of charities this may be an independent examiner, auditor or reporting accountant. More details are given in the section on legal requirements. Where such an examination has taken place, a signed and dated copy of the subsequent report should be included in the accounts.

The report of the incoming and outgoing resources of the organisation may be presented by a number of methods. Although there is an element of choice for trustees in the method that they adopt, the presentation of the accounts of registered charities and companies is determined by regulation. The different formats available for charity accounts are discussed below in the section on legal requirements.

## Balance sheet

In addition to information on the funds flowing in and out of the charity over the year, all accounts must include a balance sheet, describing the assets and liabilities at the end of the financial year. The balance sheet acts like a photograph of the charity's financial position on the day that marks the end of the financial year. A sample balance sheet is presented in the box below, but first we will look at the key elements of the balance sheet.

The balance sheet should record the charity's assets, including fixed assets (e.g. buildings and long-term investments) and current assets (i.e. cash and other assets that can be converted into cash within a 12-month period). Current assets include short-term investments, bank balances, stock, any cash in hand and debtors (i.e. those owing money to the charity). The balance sheet should also show any liabilities (money owed

**NOTE**

Charities with an annual income of £100,000 or less which chose to present their accounts in the receipts and payments format are only required to produce a simplified balance sheet. (See the following section on legal requirements.)

by the charity). These should be divided into current liabilities payable in the next 12 months (e.g. payments owed to suppliers and other creditors) and liabilities due after one year, such as mortgages and other long-term loan arrangements.

The difference between current assets and current liabilities represents the net current assets or net current liabilities, and this figure should be shown in the balance sheet.

---

**tip**

*Net current asset or liability?*
Trustees should watch out for the net current asset/net current liability figure. Net current assets show that the organisation has enough money to meet its immediate debts, whereas a net current liability indicates that there are not sufficient funds to meet debts without realising fixed assets (e.g. selling property). A net current liability figure is a clear danger sign regarding the financial health of the organisation and indicates poor financial management.

*Current asset:liability ratio*
Even where a charity has net current assets, trustees should consider the balance between current assets and current liabilities. If current assets are more or less equal to current liabilities (a ratio of 1:1), the organisation only has enough money to meet its debts and will be left with little, if any, cash once these are paid. In contrast, a 2:1 ratio, i.e. current assets which are twice the value of current liabilities, would leave the charity with cash to spare once debts are paid. A ratio of 1:2 would mean that liabilities were twice the value of the assets available to pay them.

The ratio is calculated by dividing both figures by the smaller number, so the ratio for the sample balance sheet below is:

current assets: current liabilities = £5500: £1000
divide both figures by 1000 = 5.5:1

This is a very healthy ratio.

---

The balance sheet should also show the breakdown of funds into those that are:

- unrestricted, i.e. can be used for any purpose within the objects of the charity;
- restricted, i.e. can only be used for a specific purpose; and
- designated, i.e. have been allocated to a particular purpose by the trustees.

**SAMPLE BALANCE SHEET**

*Anytown Children and Families Forum*
Balance sheet as at 31st March 2002

| | Note | 2002 | 2001 |
|---|---|---|---|
| **Fixed Assets** | | | |
| Tangible assets | 9 | 3250 | 3250 | 2000 |
| Investments | 6 | 2000 | 2000 | 2000 |
| **Total** | | **5250** | **5250** | **4000** |
| **Current assets** | | | |
| Debtors | 10 | 1500 | 1500 | 1250 |
| Cash at bank and in hand | | 4000 | 4000 | 3500 |
| **Total** | | **5500** | **5500** | **4750** |
| Creditors: | | | |
| amount falling due within one year | 11 | 1000 | 1000 | 950 |
| **Net current assets** | | **4500** | **4500** | **3800** |
| **Total assets less current liabilities** | | **9750** | **9750** | **7800** |
| **Funds** | | | |
| Unrestricted funds | | | |
| General | | 2750 | 2750 | 1800 |
| Designated | 12 | 2000 | 2000 | 2000 |
| Restricted funds | 2,3 | 5000 | 5000 | 4000 |
| **Total** | | **9750** | **9750** | **7800** |

A more detailed description of these terms will be given later in this chapter. We will also look at their significance in terms of reserves.

**Pension funds**

There are specific requirements relating to the reporting of pension funds in accounts. These are described in Financial Reporting Standard (FRS) 17. Charities with their own pension schemes should consult their professional advisers for further information.

# Legal requirements

The presentation, content and examination of charity and company accounts are determined by legislation and regulation. Charity

Commission requirements for accounts are laid down in the Statement of Recommended Practice for Accounting and Reporting by Charities (SORP) and are determined by income thresholds, with a lighter touch for smaller organisations. A table summarising the requirements for different sized charities is included at the end of this section. The regulations represent the minimum standard that must be applied by charities. A charity may decide to apply a higher standard than is required for its income band and if this standard is specified in the governing document, the charity must follow the specified standard.

Some registered charities may be subject to accounting requirements under different legislation or regulatory bodies. For example, there is a separate SORP for housing associations.

---

**CAUTION!**

The requirements of the SORP are detailed, wide ranging and sometimes complex. The precise interpretation of the regulations into your accounts will depend on the circumstances of your charity. As this book is aimed at the trustees of small to medium charities we have focussed on the key issues for those groups. More detailed guidance is available from the Charity Commission and specialist publications, some of which are listed in the Directory. Trustees should also seek professional support as necessary.

---

### Presentation and content

*Receipts and payments:* This is a simple form of presentation, summarising funds paid out and received over the year and listing remaining cash and non-cash assets and any liabilities at the end of the year. Such accounts do not give a detailed view of the organisation's finances and so are not appropriate for large organisations. Only unincorporated charities with an income of £100,000 or less may use this form of presentation.

*Accruals:* These are more detailed accounts showing a 'true and fair' record of charity finances over the year. Accruals accounts contain a full balance sheet, a statement of financial activities (known as the SOFA) and explanatory notes. Charities with an income in excess of £100,000 and all charitable companies must compile accruals accounts. The sample accounts below use the accruals presentation.

---

**CAUTION!**

Trustees of charities with an income of £100,000 or less may decide or be required by their governing document to adopt the accruals format. In such circumstances, trustees cannot take a 'pick and mix' approach to the format, rather they must fully comply with the SORP regulations.

---

## Statement of Financial Activities (SOFA)

This is the prescribed format for accruals accounting by charities. The SOFA requires charities to present incoming resources and resources expended in a columnar format showing the transactions within different funds. The accounts should include a column each for unrestricted funds, restricted funds and endowed funds and for the totals for the current and previous year. If the organisation does not have a particular type of fund, then the appropriate column does not need to be included.

---

**ANALYSIS OF FUNDS**

Charities hold their resources as unrestricted, restricted, endowed or designated funds. Accounts should clearly identify these funds. The distinction between them is as follows.

*Unrestricted funds.* These are funds that may be used for any purpose within the charity's objects. Often these funds are obtained from general donations and fundraising and income from investments. Some funders, such as local authorities, may give grants on an unrestricted basis.

*Restricted funds.* These are moneys that have been given to the charity for a specific purpose.

Where an organisation has been given a grant for a particular project or donations to work with an identified client group, these funds can only be used for the purpose for which they were given and as such are restricted. Such money cannot be used for the general administration of the charity or to finance work in another project or with a different beneficiary group.

*Endowed funds.* These are funds where there is no power to convert the capital into income, for example a gift of money given to the organisation for investment purposes on the proviso that the

*cont.*

---

---

**ANALYSIS OF FUNDS  continued**

original capital sum cannot be treated as income.

*Designated funds.* This is money that was received on an unrestricted basis that has since been allocated by the trustees to a particular purpose, e.g. a building refurbishment or new project. Because the funds were allocated by trustee decision, not by the funder, the trustees can decide to 'unallocate' them and move the money back to unrestricted funds for general use or to re-designate it to another project.

Charities are not required to report designated funds as a separate column in the SOFA, although they should be separately recorded in the balance sheet.

---

As well as standardising columns, the SOFA prescribes a standard format for the rows of the accounts. This format describes income and expenditure by its nature, followed by a total for each row for both the current and previous financial year. Incoming resources are split into:

- donations, legacies and similar income (many organisations include a separate row for grants);
- income from operating activities, with a distinction between those that further charitable objects and those that generate funds;
- investment income; and
- other incoming resources.

Resources expended are divided into charitable expenditure and the cost of generating funds. Charitable expenditure may be broken down into:

- activities that further the objects;
- grants payable;
- support costs; and
- management and administration costs.

As with the columns for funds, rows for income or expenditure that are not relevant to the charity may be omitted.

Columns should be totalled to show the net movement in funds during the year, the funds brought forward from the previous financial year and those that will be carried forward to the next. The SOFA should also show any movement between funds, such as a transfer from the general unrestricted fund into a designated fund or to cover a deficit in restricted funds.

**SAMPLE SOFA**

Anytown Children and Families Forum

Statement of Financial Activities for year ending 31st March 2002

| | Note | Unrestricted funds | Restricted funds | Total funds 2002 | Total funds 2001 |
|---|---|---|---|---|---|
| **Incoming resources** | | | | | |
| Grants | 2 | 40,000 | 31,650 | 71,650 | 65,550 |
| Incoming resources from training and consultancy fees | 3 | 21,975 | | 21,975 | 15,667 |
| Incoming resources from activities for generating funds | 4 | 5,643 | 4,983 | 10,626 | 9,861 |
| Donations | 5 | 550 | | 550 | 460 |
| Investment income | 6 | 120 | | 120 | 140 |
| **Total incoming resources** | | **68,288** | **36,633** | **104,921** | **91,678** |
| Less cost of generating funds | 4 | 981 | 763 | 1,744 | 1,871 |
| **Net incoming resources** | | **67,307** | **35,870** | **103,177** | **89,807** |
| **Charitable expenditure** | | | | | |
| Cost of charitable activities | 7 | 61,894 | 32,029 | 93,923 | 83,956 |
| Managing and administering the charity | 8 | 4,463 | 2,841 | 7,304 | 6,054 |
| **Total charitable resources expended** | | **66,357** | **34,870** | **101,227** | **90,010** |
| **Net movement in total funds for the year** | | 950 | 1,000 | 1,950 | (203) |
| Total funds brought forward | 2,3,12 | 3,800 | 4,000 | 7,800 | 8,003 |
| Total funds carried forward | 2,3,12 | 4,750 | 5,000 | 9,750 | 7,800 |

As can be seen from this example, the SOFA format provides a useful means for trustees and other readers of the accounts to monitor not just expenditure, but expenditure within different funds and between direct charitable activities and the management of the organisation.

## Notes to the accounts

As can be seen from the sample balance sheet and SOFA, accruals accounts include explanatory notes that give more details about the figures included. The first note to the accounts normally explains the organisation's accounting policy, e.g. that the accounts have been prepared on the accruals basis. The subsequent notes will include, for example, a breakdown of the different grants received and of restricted funds, their purposes and sources. Notes should also provide an explanation of any designated funds and of the value of fixed assets, including any changes in fixed asset values over the past year. The SORP requires that the following additional information is included in the notes to the accounts.

- *Related party transactions.* Any arrangements between the charity and any individual or other organisation to which it is related must be reported in the notes to the accounts. Related parties include trustees, people connected with the trustees, and organisations that are related because, for example, they have power to appoint members of the board or share a significant proportion of common trustees. Such reporting encourages transparency in managing potential conflicts of interest.
- *Payments to trustees.* Any payments to trustees from charity funds must be recorded in the accounts. Detailed disclosure is required, with payments separately recorded and the legal justification for such payments (e.g. provision within the governing document) explained. Other forms of trustee benefit, such as trustee indemnity insurance cover, should also be included.
- *Trustee expenses.* Charities do not need to declare collective trustee expenses (e.g. room hire for meetings) or reimbursement of trustees for purchases, such as stationery, made on the charity's behalf. Charities do need to record in their accounts expenses reimbursed to trustees on an individual basis in respect of costs incurred as part of their trusteeship.

- *Staffing costs.* Charities which employ staff should record in their accounts their total staffing costs, the average number of full time equivalent staff employed during the year and the number of staff receiving individual remuneration above £50,000. This should be presented as the number of staff falling into each £10,000 band from £50,000 p.a. upwards.

## Trustees' report

All registered charities are required to produce a trustees' report as part of their annual accounts. This is not the glossy annual report or the minutes of the AGM, but a breakdown of legal and administrative details and information on the work undertaken in the past year. Charities with an income below £250,000 need only produce a summary report. Those with income above £250,000 are required to supply a full report, which should cover the following information:

- name of the organisation;
- details of the legal structure (e.g. that the charity is an unincorporated association and the date on which the constitution was adopted);
- registered address;
- list of trustees;
- details of professional advisers, bankers etc.;
- compliance with legal and regulatory requirements and with the governing document;
- description of the organisational and decision-making structure;
- principal activities and any changes to those activities;
- significant developments over the past year, both positive and negative, and likely future developments;
- if there was any deficit at the beginning of the financial year, steps taken to address the deficit;
- the policies of the charity, including on reserves, investment etc.;
- the effectiveness of fundraising activities; and
- a statement describing the major risks faced by the charity and the steps taken to minimise such risks (we looked at risk management in chapter 2 and will review the subject again at the end of this chapter).

The report should be adopted by the board and signed (and dated) on their behalf by one of the trustees, usually the chairperson or secretary.

Clearly such a wide-ranging report runs the risk of becoming a lengthy and complex document. The report is intended to serve as an overview of the charity and its activities over the past year and as such trustees will need to find a balance between clarity and brevity.

Trustees of smaller charities (those with incomes of £250,000 p.a. or less) should consider the areas required in respect of the full report when preparing their summary documents.

### Examination

There are also requirements for registered bodies to have their accounts verified by an independent person. The inspection will consider whether the accounts accurately report the organisation's financial position and whether this can be substantiated by supporting information. Again, the extent of the inspection is determined by income thresholds, although the terms of an organisation's governing document may impose a standard higher than that required by the law. In determining the level of inspection, trustees should consider both the governing document and the legislation and adopt whichever standard is higher (for more information, see the section on drafting governing documents in chapter 4).

The different categories of inspection are described below.

*Audit.* This is the most onerous form of inspection and must be carried out by a qualified auditor. The intention of this form of inspection is to verify whether the accounts present a true and fair view of the organisation's financial status. The auditor will subject the financial statements to a thorough examination including a consideration of the sources of income and any restrictions on incoming resources; the allocation of expenditure and the matching of expenditure to income streams; evidence to support the financial statements; financial controls; legal compliance and analysis of risk, including fraud. The auditor will need to see a wide range of supporting documents in order to collate the information necessary to audit the accounts effectively.

Audit fees will probably have to be paid, although some local authorities do provide auditing services free of charge to local charities. Any fees can be paid from charity funds.

*Independent examination.* A lighter touch than audit, independent examination should be carried out by someone independent of the charity who the trustees have reason to believe has appropriate skills to conduct the examination. Examples include bank managers, finance officers etc., although use of a qualified accountant is recommended. The independent examination will consider whether the accounts are compliant with the SORP regulations, identify serious failures in the maintenance of accounts, and review unusual or anomalous items in the accounts.

Whatever the method of inspection, the person inspecting the accounts will produce a report on the basis of his or her examination. There are set formats for both auditors' and independent examiners' reports. This report, signed and dated by the examiner or auditor, should be included within the final copy of the accounts. Where the inspection of accounts shows everything to be in order, the accounts are termed 'clean'. Where a discrepancy has been discovered, perhaps because the organisation could not provide supporting evidence, the inspector will include this as a qualification against a clean report and the accounts will be termed as 'qualified'. Qualified accounts are often interpreted as an indicator of poor financial management and the trustees should carefully consider any advice provided by the examiner or auditor regarding the means of remedying the problems identified.

---

**tip**

Bear in mind that an independent examination is nowhere near as stringent a form of scrutiny as an audit, and consequently an examiner's report has less value than that of an auditor in terms of certifying the veracity of the accounts and the financial health of an organisation. In contrast, auditors can play a valuable role in raising the standard of charities' financial reporting and controls. Trustees who are concerned about their charity's financial status and management may do well to subject their accounts to a full audit (even if this is not legally required) as a means of monitoring the situation and identifying solutions to difficult areas.

---

### Charitable companies

Charitable companies are in the unfortunate position of being subject to both company law and charity law in terms of the presentation of accounts, although company law prevails when it comes to the examination requirements. As has already been stated, all charitable companies, regardless of income, must present their accounts under the accruals approach and, consequently, adopt the SOFA format. The SOFA has been designed to comply with the principal requirements for companies to produce income and expenditure accounts, although there may be occasions when charitable companies will need to include an additional income and expenditure account within their financial statements. Similarly, a full trustees' report will cover most of the information required for the company directors' report. Director/trustees must additionally ensure that all directors are listed in the report and that they state their compliance with company law as well as charity law. Charitable companies must file their annual report and accounts with Companies House as well as the Charity Commission.

Company law requirements for external scrutiny are less onerous than those for charities. There is no requirement for external examination for charitable companies with a gross income of less than £90,000. Charitable companies with an income of £90,001 to £250,000 may submit an audit exemption report, prepared by a reporting accountant. A full audit is required where income is over £250,000.

## Branches

In chapter 4 we looked at group structures and the sometimes complex arrangements that can exist in terms of branches. The SORP defines branches as falling within two categories: those which are part of the administration of the parent charity; and those which have a separate legal status but are administered by or on behalf of the parent body. In the latter case, branch funds will be held for the purposes of the parent charity which will in turn have significant influence over that branch.

Where branches are not autonomous entities, the SORP requires that all branch transactions, assets and liabilities should be included gross (rather than netted off) in the parent charity's accounts. Such branches may also produce their own accounts for the benefit of local supporters. Branch funds should be recorded as restricted or unrestricted funds as appropriate.

Autonomous charities which are known as branches but fall outside the above definition should prepare their own annual accounts and describe the relationship with their parent body in their trustees' report.

## Other requirements

There are some further key requirements in relation to charity accounts.

*Retention of accounts.* Financial records, including invoices and receipts as well as the accounts themselves, must be kept for three years by charitable companies and for six years by other registered charities.

*Submission of accounts.* All registered charities which have an annual income in excess of £10,000 must submit their accounts to the Charity Commission within 10 months of their financial year end. All charitable companies must also submit their accounts to Companies House within

**Minimum accounting requirements**

| Type of organisation | Presentation of accounts | Method of inspection | Trustees' report | Submission to the Commission |
|---|---|---|---|---|
| *Unincorporated charities (by annual income)* | | | | |
| £0–£10,000 | Receipts and payments | Not required | Summary | No annual return. Accounts on request. |
| £10,001– £100,000 | Receipts and payments | Independent examination | Summary | Annual return. Accounts within 10 months of year end. |
| £100,001– £250,000 | Accruals | Independent examination | Summary | Annual return. Accounts within 10 months of year end. |
| £250,001 + | Accruals | Audit | Full | Annual return. Accounts within 10 months of year end. |
| *Charitable companies (by annual income)* | | | | |
| £0–£10,000 | Accruals | No external scrutiny required | Summary | No annual return. Accounts on request. |
| £10,001– £90,000 | Accruals | No external scrutiny | Summary | Annual return. Accounts within 10 months of year end. |
| £90,000– £250,000 | Accruals | Audit exemption report (if no full audit prepared) | Full | Annual return. Accounts within 10 months of year end. |
| £250,001 + | Accruals | Audit | Full | Annual return. Accounts within 10 months of year end. |

the same period. Charities with income of £10,000 or less must submit accounts to the Commission on request. In addition, charities above the £10,000 threshold must also complete and submit the Commission's annual return, giving summary information on income and expenditure, fundraising costs, trustees and trustee benefits and the use of property (blank forms are sent to charities for completion).

*Supply of accounts.* Registered charities are required to supply their accounts to those who request them. Any financial statements distributed must include the trustees' report and any external examiner's report.

---

**CAUTION!**

Some organisations are required to include a cash flow statement in their accounts. This provision applies to large organisations with turnovers in excess of £2m, balance sheet totals of over £1m and large staff teams. As this book is aimed at small to medium charities, the requirements for cash flow statements are not discussed here. Trustees who believe that their charity may fall into this provision should seek further information.

---

**PROPOSED CHANGES – ACCOUNTING REQUIREMENTS**

The Cabinet Office Strategy Unit has proposed a range of changes to the legal requirements for charity accounts, following its review of charity law. Their recommendations include:

- improvements to the SORP that will strengthen the focus on achievements against a charity's objectives and the impact of its work;
- improved means of apportioning costs and expenditure in order that readers of accounts can make more meaningful comparisons between organisations;

- a requirement for charities to state their procedures for recruiting, inducting and training new trustees.

None of these changes would require legislative change. The Unit also recommends that the thresholds for examination of charity accounts should be changed. It proposes that charities with an income of between £10,000 and £1m should have their accounts independently examined, whilst those with a total annual income in excess of £1m should have their accounts professionally audited. In addition, it recommends

*cont.*

---

**PROPOSED CHANGES – ACCOUNTING REQUIREMENTS continued**

that charities with incomes of over £1m should:

- declare their ethical investment stance in their annual reports; and
- complete an annual 'standard information return', focussing on how the charity sets its objectives and measures the outcomes of its work. This information would be made available to the public via the Charity Commission website.

The change in accounting thresholds and the requirement to declare charities' positions in relation to ethical investment would require legislative change.

---

## Funders' requirements

Some funders may also place requirements on the recording of their grants in the accounts. For example it may be a condition of the grant that income and expenditure under the agreement is separately identified, labelled in a certain way and recorded as a restricted fund.

## Accounts as a tool for trustees

The need to produce accounts goes far beyond the mere legal requirement. Accounts are a vital means of representing the financial position of the charity to external organisations and to the trustees. They allow trustees to monitor the charity's financial progress, or otherwise, on an annual basis, helping them to make decisions regarding the need to develop or scale down activities, reduce liabilities, increase assets, spend balances or raise extra funds. Breakdowns of income and expenditure can inform decisions regarding diversifying sources of funding, developing or curtailing certain fundraising activities and extending operational activities. The requirement to produce reports on an annual basis also impacts on the management and control of day-to-day finances insofar as trustees will need to be able to retrieve the information necessary to produce accurate annual accounts.

# Management accounts

So far we have looked at annual accounts. Whilst annual accounts are useful for trustees in reflecting on the current financial position and long-term planning, their infrequency makes them less useful in ensuring financial viability on a day-to-day basis. Once the end of the financial year has arrived, it may be too late. This where management accounts may prove valuable. Management accounts, usually produced monthly, are an essential tool for trustees and senior staff in monitoring ongoing expenditure.

## Establishing cost centres

Bald indicators of income and expenditure are of limited help as a day-to-day management tool. Instead, trustees need to know where income is being spent and whether this expenditure reflects their intentions. To do this, the trustees need to establish cost centres. Cost centres are areas of expenditure or items that are grouped together for the purpose of budget setting and monitoring expenditure. Small, single function organisations are unlikely to have many separate cost centres, but organisations running multiple projects or in receipt of restricted funds will need to have more complex arrangements in place. For example, there might be a cost centre for each project or a cost centre for each restricted fund. This allows the trustees to monitor income and expenditure in different areas of the organisation, pinpointing issues of concern. Within each cost centre there are likely to be common elements, e.g. travel expenses, training costs, running expenses, salaries etc.

Trustees should look at the work of the organisation as a whole and identify those areas that can be divided into cost centres and establish budget areas, e.g. salaries, travel expenses etc., within each cost centre.

## Setting and controlling budgets

Once cost centres have been identified, trustees should set budgets for each one. Although staff often play a key role in budgeting, the final responsibility for budgets rests with the trustees so the board must scrutinise this area carefully to ensure that income targets are realistic and planned expenditure is appropriate and within the charity's objects, powers and resources.

Budget setting involves considering the activities undertaken within each cost centre, the likely cost of each activity, and the resources available. This is obviously easier where a cost centre is well established and trustees can use previous expenditure as a foundation for future budgets, considering item by item whether the next year's activities will cost more, less or a similar amount and whether any additional items should be included. It is also easier where a cost centre is fully funded, for example by a specific grant or contract, as trustees will know the exact amount available for that work. In all other cases, the trustees will have to strike a balance between the costs of the activities and realistic fundraising targets. It is dangerous to set a budget based on unattainable fundraising targets. In contrast, budgets based solely on secured income can be unduly restrictive, particularly in cases where the organisation has a good track record of raising additional funds.

When setting budgets for a new activity or a new organisation, look at the expenditure of similar projects and groups as well as researching the costs of individual items, such as any necessary capital equipment, rental charges for premises, salary levels etc.

The collective total of the different cost centres represents the budget for the organisation as a whole. Budgets are commonly set on an annual basis, but within this figure, the budgets for each funding item for each cost centre should be broken down on a monthly basis. This information allows trustees to use management accounts as a monitoring tool. Some budget items may be easily split into one-twelfth to represent each month's planned expenditure. For example, static costs such as salaries and rent will stay the same each month. There may be other items that are seasonal, annual, bi-monthly or quarterly, such as training fees, insurance premiums and special events. Costs for these items should be included within the breakdown under the appropriate month or months.

**tip**

Month by month budgeting can help in managing cash flow and investments as it will illustrate how much money is needed at any given point in the year.

Management accounts may then show, by cost centre, and within cost centre by item:

- budget for the month;
- expenditure for the month;
- budget to date;
- expenditure to date; and
- annual budget.

Trustees can then measure overspends and underspends against each item. This gives a much better understanding of organisational finances and allows greater control over expenditure to be exercised. As part of the budget setting exercise, trustees may identify performance indicators or other forms of measurement that will clearly signal to the board whether the finances are healthy or in danger. Such performance indicators will be linked to organisational objectives and may include, for example, spending to target, reducing expenditure in some areas (e.g. office costs) and/or increasing expenditure in others (e.g. grants to beneficiaries or staff training). The combination of detailed budgeting and performance measures helps trustees to ask the right questions regarding variations from budget. Does an underspend represent a lack of activity? Why have overspends occurred in certain areas? Can budgets be revised to move funds from underspending areas to new developments? Is income generation on target and on time? Why are some cost centres spending more than others on common budget items, such as telephone and office costs?

Cost centres such as these obviously require fairly sophisticated daily financial management, as each item of income or expenditure needs to be recorded against a cost centre and budget heading within that centre. The benefits do justify the effort. As has been seen above, the trustees gain useful information and it also allows them to delegate an appropriate degree of financial control to staff. For example, a project manager may be given spending authority within the cost centre for the project, without being able to sign off expenditure in other areas of the organisation.

## Financial controls

Documented and implemented financial controls are crucial to the proper governance of any organisation, regardless of its size or sector. For charity trustees, financial controls are the means by which they retain a meaningful responsibility for organisational finances. Such controls support accurate financial reporting, provide a means by which trustees can demonstrate financial probity and, critically, are a key weapon in preventing fraud. As such, financial controls should be developed in every charity, including those run entirely by the trustees.

Financial controls determine the way in which all funds of the organisation are handled, governing both the process of receiving and spending money and the authorities within the organisation to make financial decisions. Basic principles include:

- spreading responsibility across a range of individuals, for example through arrangements for checking or countersigning transactions (on the premise that vesting too much responsibility in one person heightens the risk of abuse);
- detailed recording of all transactions; and
- escalating spending authorities within the organisation, so that all expenditure over a certain level has to be signed off by trustees.

Trustees should develop a written financial control policy. Trustees and any staff or volunteers who have financial responsibilities should be aware of the contents of the policy and apply its requirements consistently. The procedure should cover the following areas:

## Spending authority

Who will have authority to make payments from the charity's funds? The following are common scenarios.

1 In small organisations it may be that the trustees decide not to delegate any authority to staff or volunteers in respect of spending charitable funds. It is still necessary to consider whether, for example, two trustees can authorise expenditure up to a certain threshold but expenditure above the threshold must be endorsed by the full board.

2 In charities with a small staff team, staff can often authorise expenditure up to the first threshold, a member of staff together with a trustee can authorise expenditure up to the second threshold, but any expenditure above that level must be approved by two trustees and, ultimately, the whole trustee board.

3 In larger organisations, different staff may have spending authority within their own cost centres, with senior employees such as the chief executive or finance manager having overall authorities. In such circumstances, staff with cost centre spending authority will usually be subject to an upper threshold before the expenditure has to be approved by one of the senior employees. Some funders do not like these arrangements, and may require that expenditure over a certain amount has to have trustee authorisation.

Whatever the model adopted, some basic principles apply:

- only the trustees should have authority to endorse expenditure that is outside the budget or above a certain level;

- no payment should be released on the approval of one person alone, instead every expenditure should be countersigned by another person with appropriate spending authority;
- nobody should have authority to approve payments to themselves or to some other individual or organisation in which they have an interest, e.g. staff and trustees should not be able to sign off their own expenses; and
- two people from the same family or household should not have authority to authorise the same expenditure (e.g. they should not be able to sign the same cheque).

## Setting spending authorities

We have not suggested threshold levels for spending authorities because these are very individual to the charity. Issues to consider include the level of spending authority relative to the charity's budget, the need (if any) to access money quickly, the level and frequency of expenditure and the role of individual staff members. For example, a small charity with a lone worker carrying out administrative functions may limit that worker's spending authority to, for example, £25 to cover the cost of stationery. A multi-million pound charity with a professionally qualified and highly experienced senior management team may give senior management a spending authority of £100,000 provided that the expenditure has been budgeted for. If employees' job descriptions include an element of management, especially financial management, and they have been recruited for these skills, then it is likely to be appropriate that such posts should carry a degree of spending authority.

If the nature of the charity's work means that spending is limited to regular and predictable items such as salaries, rent and utilities, there may be no need for the trustees to delegate any control. In contrast, other charities may have frequent calls on their finances that, although within budget, are unpredictable and urgent. For example, a charity providing crisis grants or loans to its clients will need to delegate spending authority to those working with the beneficiaries.

## Documentation

*Record keeping.* Records should be kept of all money received and spent. These records should include basic information such as the amount, from whom the money was received or to whom it was paid; and the date and purpose of the transaction. Any documentation such as receipts and invoices should be retained. Each transaction should be recorded against the appropriate cost centre and budget heading within that cost centre. Records should be reconciled against balances, with no single person responsible for record keeping. Instead, all records should be checked by one other person. In small charities the responsibility is often spilt between the senior member of staff and the treasurer.

*Cheques.* All organisations should require two signatures on each cheque as a means of verifying the genuine purpose of the payment. Cheque signatories should be authorised in line with the organisation's spending authorities. Some charities have difficulties with cheque payments because of problems in bringing cheque signatories together and attempt to address this by asking one of the signatories to pre-sign blank cheques. This completely undermines the value of the joint signing arrangements and lays the charity wide open to cheque fraud. If arranging joint signatures is a problem, review spending authorities and see if the availability of signatories can be approved by, for example, adding an additional signatory to the list.

*Handling cash.* Cash transactions represent an area of charity finance that is extremely vulnerable to abuse. Organisations are advised to avoid cash transactions as far as possible. Where they are unavoidable, for example in relation to voluntary donations, organisations should make sure that a stringent process is in place for the documentation of cash transactions and witnessed recording. For example, opening of post or opening collecting tins should be witnessed by a second person and any cash recorded. Receipts should be given to all those paying cash to the organisation and copies of receipts should be kept. Any cash payments in respect of expenses should be provided only upon receipt of appropriate evidence (e.g. bus tickets, mileage forms etc.) and should be properly recorded. If it is necessary to keep petty cash, again any expenditure must

**ESSENTIALS**

NEVER release funds without appropriate documentation.
ALWAYS issue receipts for funds received.
ALWAYS record all financial transactions.

be documented and trustees should specify a maximum float. Safe arrangements should be made for the storage of cash, with access details known only to a limited number of people.

## Reserves

Many charities struggle to raise cash, with wealthy voluntary groups being in the lucky minority, but whether cash-strapped or cash-rich, charities should consider the level of funds they will require as a safety net in case normal funding sources dry up or expenses unexpectedly rise. These safety net or rainy day funds are the charity's reserves, i.e. the income funds that are freely available to the charity for its general purposes, once it has met its financial commitments and provided for other planned expenditure. Although for many charities, talk of high levels of reserves will be a pipe dream, trustees should consider the function of the funds they hold, which can result in a delicate balancing act between organisational prudence and furthering charitable objectives. Funds given for charitable purposes must be spent on charitable purposes rather than hoarded for some future, unidentified eventuality; consequently, the holding of funds in reserve without justification may amount to a breach of trust. At the same time trustees have an obligation to act in the best interests of the charity as an organisation. This will inevitably involve maintaining a healthy cashflow and adequate funds to meet future liabilities. The Charity Commission recognises the need to maintain such a balance and so expects trustees to develop a reserves policy that identifies the purpose and amount of reserves held or desirable in order to justify the retention of charitable funds. The SORP requires that this policy is discussed in the trustees' report within charities' annual accounts.

**tip**

If your reserves sit at a level higher than that needed to fulfil your organisation's charitable purposes and meet any future financial commitments, you should contact the Charity Commission. A possible solution is a Commission Scheme to extend the objects of your charity, e.g. by increasing the area of benefit. Trustees have a legal duty to apply for a Scheme where this is an appropriate course of action.

## Developing your reserves policy

Reserves policies will differ between organisations depending on the nature of their activities, financial commitments, potential liabilities and future plans, including any plans to develop services, forecasts of income and expenditure and reliability of income sources.

- If an organisation plans future expansion, for example through the purchase of a new property or development of a new project, the trustees may include within the reserves policy the allocation of a proportion of current assets to a designated fund for this purpose. This acts very much like a personal savings account and the trustees may set a target figure to be attained by a certain date through an annual allocation to the designated fund. Designated funds are not always included in the total figure for reserves.

- If the charity already owns a building, it may allocate a proportion of funds from its assets, in addition to its annual maintenance budget, to expenditure on unexpected maintenance tasks that will not be covered by insurance. It may also know of forthcoming maintenance tasks, such as repainting, that do not form part of the annual budget but can be provided for through a reserves policy.

- Trustees will also need to look at the balance between financial security and commitments. Have the trustees entered into any contractual arrangements that extend beyond the period of secured funding? These may include property and equipment leases and staff employment contracts. The reserves policy should include provision for meeting liabilities under these contracts should funding cease, for example by including sums to cover break clause penalties and redundancy payments. In contrast, if an organisation has secure funding for a three-year project, risks will be much lower and the approach to reserves should reflect this.

- Many reserves policies include provision for rescue or run-down time in the event of funding ceasing. This may be anything between 3 to 12 months' running costs and allows time for the charity to continue operating whilst seeking alternative funding and, if unsuccessful, for the charity to be wound up in a way that minimises disruption and meets liabilities.

Taking these different elements together, you will be able to identify why you need reserves and a target figure for reserves. These factors should form the basis of the policy, even if the target figure is currently unattainable. You should then look at how these funds will be made up. For charities without fixed assets, this is simple. Reserves can only be cash and investments. For charities with property the issue is slightly different. For example, it may be possible to realise cash through mortgages (although the charity must be in a position to repay them). Where the property is not used for the delivery of the charity's services (e.g. it is rented to a third party), it may be possible to use the value of that property within the reserves sum as its sale would not affect the functioning of the organisation. Where the property is key to organisational activities, such as a day care centre, the value of the property could be included in that part of the reserves policy which considers liabilities on closure of the charity.

Organisations with inadequate funds to achieve their ideal reserves policy may operate a two-tier approach, keeping the overall policy as a target to aim for and commit any operating surplus to, whilst running a more modest achievable policy. These modest policies usually relate to cash flow and immediate liabilities. For example, an charity may have a policy of not taking on liabilities that cannot be met from current cash resources (rather than next month's grant cheque) and maintaining adequate current assets to meet running costs for the next three months.

The charity's activities and financial obligations will inevitably change over time, so the reserves policy should include details of how the policy itself will be monitored and reviewed.

### Calculating the level of reserves

There are different methods of calculating reserves and the method chosen should be determined within your reserves policy and applied consistently. The definition used in the SORP is described in the box on p. 154. However, trustees should be aware that funders may adopt a different approach to that of the Charity Commission, e.g. by including designated funds within the reserves figure.

### Reserves and funding applications

Funding bodies, and some canny individual donors, will look at charities' reserves levels. After all, why should they give money for a project or expense that the charity could afford to cover itself? On the other hand,

## CALCULATING RESERVES

The SORP defines reserves as income which is available to the charity and can be spent at the trustees' discretion in furthering charitable objects but which is not yet spent, committed or designated. Under this definition, permanent and expendable endowments, restricted and designated funds, and income funds which could only be accessed by disposing of fixed assets held for charity use, are excluded from the calculation of reserves.

Reserves can, therefore, be calculated as follows:

Net assets (i.e. all assets minus all liabilities)
Minus tangible fixed assets
Minus endowments
Minus restricted funds
Minus designated funds
= Free Reserves

When calculating your level of reserves, be careful not to 'double minus' any of the figures. We can illustrate this problem by using the sample balance sheet considered earlier in this chapter. Using this formula, free reserves would be calculated as follows:

£9750 net assets
− £3250 fixed assets
− £2000 designated fund
− £5000 restricted fund
= − £500 free reserves

This calculation has resulted in a negative free reserves figure, however if the fixed assets represent part of the restricted funds, their value will have been double counted in the calculation. The true reserves figure would look more like this:

£9750 net assets
− £2000 designated fund
− £5000 restricted fund (including £3250 fixed assets)
= £2750 free reserves

The period, in weeks, of running costs that this figure represents can be calculated using the following equation:

reserves
divided by unrestricted expenditure for the year
multiplied by 52
= number of weeks running costs.

From our sample balance sheet

$$\frac{£2750}{£66,357} \times 52$$

= 2 weeks' running costs

would they want to give money to a charity that could fold at any moment? For these reasons, in addition to the SORP requirements, charities need to have a reserves policy in place and to be able to communicate it to potential funders. High levels of reserves may be completely justifiable if the organisation is committing significant amounts of its own money to the project or would have heavy financial commitments in the event of closure, just as non-existent reserves may be acceptable if the organisation is tightly funded but maintains a good cashflow.

**CAUTION!**

Never include restricted funds in your reserves figure. Restricted funds may only be used for the purpose for which they were given. Charities cannot use these funds for any other purpose, even in order to bail them out of a difficult situation. If they do, they may be required to return the funds to the original intended purpose or repay the misspent amount to the funder.

## Cashflow forecasts

In the last section we talked about cashflow in the context of reserves. A good cashflow would ensure that the organisation is always able to pay its bills and meet immediate liabilities. A poor cashflow would result in overdrafts and other forms of debt and late payments of bills, incurring interest and other penalty charges. As well as being financially damaging, poor cashflow may harm the charity's reputation and its relationships with creditors, be they external suppliers or internal creditors, such as staff.

Cashflow can be managed through a cashflow forecast. This plans 'money in' and 'money out', allowing organisations to assess their financial viability on an ongoing basis, planning the best timing for expenditure, avoiding the need for overdrafts or short-term loans and maximising the benefits of available funds by investing spare cash wherever possible. A tool that should be used by all organisations, cash flow forecasts are particularly valuable for charities on tight budgets with limited reserves and new charities and projects that have yet to develop an established spending cycle or back-up funds.

### Producing a cashflow forecast

As a planning tool for voluntary organisations, cashflow forecasts should cover a 12-month period with a month-by-month breakdown of resources coming into and out of the organisation or project account. It should consider the balance (and thus the availability of cash) on a monthly and cumulative basis. The forecast should start with any balances available at the beginning of the year, with the figures for the forthcoming year heavily based on the budget. Any fixed income and expenditure, such as grant payments and salaries should be included, before adding any variables. Through this method, trustees may be able to identify payments that should be rescheduled to another time of year when more resources are available, or the best time to run a large fundraising event in terms of maintaining positive cash balances. They may also be able to identify periods of surplus that present short-term investment opportunities.

A sample cashflow for the Anytown Children and Families Forum is given opposite.

## Managing funds

Trustees have an obligation to maximise the funds available to be applied to charitable causes. This is not limited to raising money, but includes management of the funds that the charity already has. In the previous section we looked at using cashflow forecasts to minimise debts incurred across the year and referred to the opportunities that may be presented for trustees to increase resources by investing spare cash on a month by month basis. Structures can be established to enable trustees to manage resources even more effectively. The obvious example is the selection of appropriate bank or building society accounts to gain the most interest on funds held. Within each month, income and expenditure can be managed to exploit such arrangements. For example, many grants are paid quarterly, but payments against that grant will be made at various stages throughout the quarter, so funds should be placed appropriately during that period. The same is true of income that is received at the beginning of the month but not paid out until the end. For example, trustees may collect fee or rental income at the beginning of the month and hold those sums for four weeks before using them to part-fund salary payments at the end of the month. Investment of charitable funds is discussed in more detail in chapter 8.

Other opportunities should also be considered, such as the availability of direct debit payments and their impact in terms of bottom line expenditure and cash flow planning.

## Sample Cashflow – Anytown Children and Families Forum

|  | Apr | May | June | July | Aug | Sept | Oct | Nov | Dec | Jan | Feb | Mar |
|---|---|---|---|---|---|---|---|---|---|---|---|---|
| **Income** | | | | | | | | | | | | |
| Local Authority grant | 6000 | | | 6000 | | | 6000 | | | 6000 | | |
| Lottery grant | | 5000 | | | 5000 | | | 5000 | | | 5000 | |
| Donations | 20 | 20 | 40 | 40 | 10 | 30 | 50 | 40 | 100 | 50 | 10 | 10 |
| Fundraising events | | | 500 | 600 | | | 250 | | 600 | | | |
| Fees | 200 | 300 | 300 | 200 | | 200 | 300 | 300 | 200 | 250 | 300 | 300 |
| Total income | 6220 | 5320 | 840 | 6840 | 5010 | 230 | 6600 | 5340 | 900 | 6300 | 5800 | 310 |
| **Expenditure** | | | | | | | | | | | | |
| Salaries | 3000 | 3000 | 3000 | 3000 | 3000 | 3000 | 3000 | 3000 | 3000 | 3000 | 3000 | 3000 |
| Rent & Running costs | 800 | 800 | 800 | 800 | 2000 | 800 | 800 | 800 | 800 | 800 | 800 | 800 |
| Subscriptions | 200 | | | 100 | | | 2000 | | | | | |
| Events | | 150 | 50 | | | 50 | 25 | 100 | 100 | | | |
| Total expenditure | 3820 | 3950 | 3850 | 3900 | 5000 | 3850 | 5825 | 3900 | 3900 | 3800 | 3800 | 3800 |
| Monthly balance | 2400 | 1370 | –3010 | 2940 | 10 | –3620 | 775 | 1440 | –3000 | 2500 | 2000 | –3490 |
| Cumulative balance (open £2000) | 4400 | 5770 | 2760 | 5700 | 5710 | 2090 | 2865 | 4305 | 1305 | 3805 | 5805 | 2315 |

## Risk management

Given trustees' legal responsibilities towards their charities, it has long been a matter of good governance practice for trustees to assess and manage any risks to the charity. As discussed earlier in this chapter, the SORP now requires a statement on the management of major risks to be included in the trustees' report. We looked at the broader concepts of risk management in chapter 2. Throughout this chapter we have discussed measures to control risk directly in relation to financial stability.

Obviously when considering financial risk, the worst case scenario for a charity is insolvency. However there are many other, less devastating but more frequent, financial risks that need to be managed by the trustees. These include:

- budget deficits;
- a drop in income;
- inability to pay liabilities in time (this does not necessarily make an organisation insolvent);
- theft of charitable funds;
- breach of trust through incorrect use of charitable funds;
- loss of a grant due to incorrect expenditure of restricted funds or some other failure to meet grant terms and conditions; and
- legal action against the charity due to negligence or breach of contract.

As we discussed in chapter 2, trustees need to consider the likelihood of the risk and the impact on the charity, should it occur, in order to decide whether managing the risk is a priority. Obviously, a charity facing imminent insolvency needs to address that risk immediately. Except in extreme circumstances, charities that have been effectively 'risk managed' by trustees should not face such a situation, because trustees will already have tackled the root problems, such as budget deficits and declining income.

The financial management practices discussed in this chapter are a crucial element of any financial risk management strategy. Effective financial reporting will act as an early warning system to trustees of financial troubles ahead. As such, they can help trustees analyse and prioritise different risks. Similarly, budget setting allows trustees to tackle problems of falling resources and budget deficits whilst proper financial controls will reduce risks in relation to misspent funds and theft.

Other risks, such as conflicts of interest, failures of health and safety and employment disputes can also have a financial impact on charities, especially if compensation is sought. Trustees must manage such risks to reduce the likelihood of them occurring, but should also consider mitigating the financial ill-effects if they do occur, for example by arranging appropriate insurance cover. Insurance is discussed in more detail in chapter 2.

# 8    Taxation and other financial issues

## INTRODUCTION

For trustees who are not financially minded, taxation, trading and investment can often be difficult areas of governance. Even if you do not feel out of your depth, it is particularly important to seek professional advice on complex financial issues in order to support the board in securing the best outcome for your charity. Yet no matter how competent and trusted your financial advisers are, you need a basic understanding of these issues. Trustees need sufficient knowledge to know when to call on specialist advice, to ask the right questions of professional advisers, to make informed decisions on policy issues, and to exercise their legal responsibility towards the charity's finances. This chapter cannot give definitive answers to complex financial queries as so much depends on the circumstances of the charity and the prevailing economic climate. Instead it aims to give you adequate knowledge to make you alert to the issues and help you to ask the right questions.

## Tax

It is a common misconception that charities do not pay tax. Whilst charities do enjoy a range of tax concessions, it is simply not true to state that charities do not pay tax at all. In this section we will look at some of the key issues trustees need to consider in terms of taxation.

There is no distinction for tax or VAT purposes between registered charities and charitable bodies that are not registered with the Charity Commission. Unregistered charities which wish to claim tax or VAT relief will need to demonstrate their charitable status to the Inland Revenue and/or HM Customs & Excise, based on the charity's objects, as described in the governing document.

> **CAUTION!**
>
> Trustees should be aware that taxation is a complex issue and the nature of each charity's activities will greatly influence the application of the law and its effect on the charity's tax burden. For this reason, trustees are advised to seek professional advice on tax issues.
>
> In addition, tax and VAT provisions are subject to regular review, particularly in terms of changes to thresholds etc. so always check the most up-to-date requirements with the Inland Revenue and/or HM Customs & Excise.

## Exemptions

The following tax exemptions are available to charities:

1  profits in relation to income from land, although some exceptions exist in relation to the purchase and sale of land;
2  income from certain trading activities (see the discussion in this chapter on trading); and
3  capital gains tax is not payable, provided that the gains are spent on charitable purposes.

This means that charities can claim back income tax that has been deducted from certain types of charity income, e.g. bank and building society interest.

The amount of tax that a charity is exempted may be restricted if the charity has not spent all of its income or gains on charitable activity.

## Donations

One of the tax concessions available to charities is the ability to receive tax-efficient donations, either through donations made before tax has been deducted (payroll giving) or through reclaiming tax on donations under the gift aid system.

*Payroll giving.* Payroll giving is a system whereby individuals make donations to charity that are deducted directly from their pay or occupational pension. The donations are taken by the employer from the employee's gross pay, before tax deductions are made, and thus no income tax is paid on the donation element of the salary. Donations are passed to an agency charity which distributes the funds to the charities nominated by the employees. There is no limit on the value of an individual employee's donations.

Trustees of charities receiving donations under payroll giving should be wary of offering benefits to donors as this may disqualify the donation from relief under the scheme. Benefits of negligible financial value, such as stickers or newsletters, are normally acceptable within the scheme.

*Gift aid.* The gift aid scheme provides for flexible tax-efficient donations to charities. Gift aid is available in respect of monetary donations (rather than gifts in kind) from tax-paying individuals and from companies.

- In the case of individuals, the charity can claim back the basic rate tax paid in respect of the donation whilst the donor can claim back the difference between the basic rate tax paid and any higher rate of tax that was paid in relation to the donation.
- Gift aid donations from companies are paid without deduction of income tax. Unlike the requirements for individual donors, no declaration is required and the charity only needs to keep the accounting records necessary to record donations. Company donors should retain any correspondence as evidence of the donation.

There are no limits on the size or number of gift aid donations although there is a requirement for charities to maintain an audit trail, documenting the source and value of the donations. More information is given on this below, when the gift aid declaration is considered. However, trustees should consider the administrative costs of reclaiming the tax on donations and may want to introduce a self-imposed minimum level below which donations will be accepted but the tax will not be reclaimed.

*Gift aid declaration.* In order to reclaim tax on a donation, charities must obtain a gift aid declaration from the donor. Although the Inland Revenue has produced a model form, there is no prescribed format for the declaration. Declarations may be made before, at the time of, or after the donation, and may cover single or multiple donations. The declaration may be given in writing (including fax and e-mail) or orally and should contain the following information:

- name and home address of the donor;
- the name of the charity;
- a description of the donations covered by the declaration, e.g. a single donation or all donations from a certain date onwards; and

- a declaration that donations are to be treated as gift aid donations. Written declarations should also contain a note explaining that the donor must pay income tax and/or capital gains tax equivalent to the tax deducted from donations.

Although there is no requirement for the declaration to be signed and dated it is good practice to do so and a date will be essential if it defines the donations made under the scheme.

If the charity receives an oral gift aid declaration it should follow this up in writing by sending the donor a record of the declaration. This should include the details provided by the donor in the declaration, the date of the donation and of the charity's written confirmation, together with notes relating to the tax requirements and the donor's right to cancel the declaration within 30 days. Oral declarations are not effective until the written record has been sent.

For sponsored events, forms can be designed that serve as a gift aid declaration for each sponsor. The declaration can be placed at the top of each sheet, with an opt-in box for sponsors to tick if they want their donation to be treated as gift aid. The form should include each sponsor's full name and home address, the amount pledged and paid, the date each donation was made and the total handed over to the charity. A model form is available from the Inland Revenue.

Donors may cancel their declarations through any means. Cancellations will be effective from the date of notification or some future date identified by the donor. Retrospective cancellations are only effective during the 30 day 'cooling off' period after written confirmation has been sent in respect of an oral declaration.

Charities need to keep documentary evidence to support their tax claims. In particular they must be able to show how much has been received from each donor. There is no set format for storing this information and charities will need to develop procedures that are compatible with their other administrative systems.

Funds given to charities for the provision of services or some other form of significant benefit will not qualify under the gift aid scheme although limited benefits to gift aid donors are acceptable.

A gift aid toolkit is available from the Inland Revenue.

*Shares.* There is provision for those who donate certain shares to charities to reclaim some tax in relation to those shares. There is also time limited provision for charities to claim 'tax credit transitional relief'

(TCTR) on dividends paid to them by UK companies in which they have shares. This relief is set at a diminishing rate and will cease altogether in April 2004.

## Claiming tax refunds

Charities must reclaim tax on the prescribed forms provided by the Inland Revenue. In addition to the reclaimed tax, the Inland Revenue will calculate and refund any interest payable.

## VAT

Value added tax (VAT) is a tax on the supply of goods and services in the UK and the Isle of Man. VAT is charged at either:
- standard rate (this applies to most goods and services);
- reduced rate (for example on fuel and power); or
- zero rate (e.g. food and books).

The supply of goods and services that are subject to these rates of VAT are the taxable supplies. There are also exempt supplies, which are not subject to VAT.

Organisations are required to register for VAT if the total financial value of their 'business' activities which are subject to VAT reaches the registration threshold. In this context 'business' is not restricted to those activities which are profit making, but includes:

1 activities involving the supply of good or services for consideration (i.e. payment in either money or kind);
2 frequent or significant activities; and
3 activities that continue over a period of time.

Charitable activities may, therefore, be counted as business activities or supplies. (The table on pp. 166–168 describes the charitable activities that are subject to VAT.) Those business supplies that are subject to VAT at any of the three rates are the organisation's taxable supplies and it is the measurement of the turnover of the taxable supplies against the registration threshold that determines whether the organisation should register for VAT. The registration threshold may change but in recent years has been around £54,000.

The amount of VAT paid to HM Customs & Excise is determined by the difference between input tax and output tax.

*Output tax.* This is the VAT charged on standard and reduced rate supplies.

*Input tax.* This is the VAT paid on purchases in relation to the taxable supplies.

If the output tax is greater than the input tax, the charity must pay the difference to HM Customs & Excise. If the charity has paid more input tax than it has charged as output tax, then it may claim the difference back. The amounts are submitted to HM Customs & Excise on a VAT return.

Input tax paid by charities in relation to goods and services connected to the charity's non-business and exempt activities cannot be offset against output tax or reclaimed.

Clearly, extensive documentation is required to account for input and output tax and to support the VAT return. The VAT paid on input supplies can only be claimed back if the charity is VAT registered. It is possible for organisations falling below the threshold to register voluntarily but trustees will need to consider whether the charity will be able to reclaim any tax, and balance the financial benefit against the corresponding administrative burden.

## Business or non-business?

As can be seen from the discussion above, it is essential for trustees to assess the services offered by their charity and to consider which elements represent business activities and whether the value of these activities crosses the registration threshold, requiring the charity to register. Unfortunately, some of the distinctions between business and non-business activity are very fine. In addition, although some charitable activity is considered business, the supplies in question may be either zero rated or exempt from VAT. The table on pp. 166–168 gives an overview of the provisions. Trustees who believe that their charity may be required to be VAT registered should seek further advice, for example by contacting their local HM Customs & Excise office.

| Activity | Business | Non-business |
|---|---|---|
| Donations, bequests and grants (that are not linked to service provision) | | Voluntary contributions and grants for which there is no subsequent reward are non-business and outside the scope of VAT, income and corporation tax. |
| Voluntary services provided without charge | | Free services are non-business activities, e.g. first aid, sea rescue and worship. Any genuine donations freely given by the recipients of these services are outside the scope of VAT. |
| Sale of donated goods (including charity shops) | The sale of donated goods is a business activity. Sales will be standard rated unless zero rated due to the nature of the product. More significantly, sales will be zero rated when made by a charity or by a taxable person who gifts the profit of the sale to a charity. | |
| Hire of charity-run buildings (for example village halls) | The hire of a charity-run building for a fee is a business. This includes village halls and other community buildings. The fee is normally exempt from VAT unless the charity chooses to waive the exemption, allowing it to register and recover input tax. The exemption cannot be waived for lets to | |

| Activity | Business | Non-business |
|---|---|---|
| | another charity for non-business use. | |
| Welfare services (including spiritual welfare) | Welfare services supplied by charities, together with any related goods, are business but are exempt provided the supplies are not made for profit, i.e. any surplus made is reinvested in the same service. If the surplus was used for a different charitable activity, the supply of welfare would be standard rated. | The same services are non-business when they are consistently supplied below cost (i.e. subsidised by at least 15 per cent from the charity's funds) to relieve the distress of beneficiaries. |
| Membership subscriptions | If members receive benefits in return for their subscriptions, e.g. publications, advice services or events, then the subscriptions will be considered to be business and subject to VAT. | Subscriptions are non-business if the members are entitled to nothing more than copies of statutory documents (i.e. annual reports and accounts) and voting rights at general meetings. |
| Corporate sponsorship | Sponsorship from companies and other bodies is subject to the standard rate of VAT if the funds are conditional on some benefit, such as the publication of the organisation's logo. In these circumstances the funds are regarded as payment for the supply of services by the charity. The fundraising exemption | Corporate donations are outside the scope of VAT if there is no reciprocal benefit. |

| Activity | Business | Non-business |
|---|---|---|
| | (see below) will apply to sponsorship in relation to one-off events. | |
| Sales of advertising in charity publications | If less than 50 per cent of advertisements in the publication represent donations from private individuals, the income from all the adverts will be subject to standard rate VAT. The supply of advertising to a charity may be zero rated and the publication may be exempt if it is part of a one-off fundraising event. | If 50 per cent or more of the advertisements printed in the publication are clearly from private individuals, the income may be treated as donations and outside the scope of VAT. |
| Interest payments | | Interest earned on funds kept in bank and building society accounts is non-business. |
| Share transactions | | The purchase and sale of shares by a charity and the receipt of dividends are not business activities. Any VAT incurred is not input tax and cannot be reclaimed. |

## Zero rated supplies to charities

A number of supplies made to charities are zero rated, meaning the charity does not have to pay any VAT on the goods and services in question. In these circumstances, the onus is on the charity to provide the supplier with a written declaration of its eligibility for zero rating on the supplies in question.

Zero rating is available on the following:

- advertising for fundraising purposes or to publicise the objectives of the charity. The zero-rating applies to advertisements in print media (including artwork and typesetting) and broadcast advertising (advertising fee only);
- recording and playback equipment for the production of talking books and newspapers for people with visual impairments (cassette tapes are standard rated);
- supply, repair, maintenance and importation of sea rescue equipment;
- construction of new self-contained buildings and annexes, excluding professional services, which are standard rated; and
- the purchase of a freehold or leasehold (exceeding 21 years) where the property will be used for a relevant charitable or residential purpose.

## Fundraising events

As has been mentioned in the table above, fundraising events may be exempt from VAT. The exemption applies to events that meet the following criteria:

1. The event must be organised and promoted primarily to raise money for the benefit of the charity.
2. The people attending the event must be aware of the fundraising purpose.
3. The event must not be part of continuous or semi-regular activities (frequent events would represent trading and not qualify for the exemption). In effect, this means that charities are limited to holding 15 events of the same kind in the same location in each financial year, although more frequent small-scale events (where gross weekly income does not exceed £1,000) are acceptable. Trustees should be aware that small-scale events taking place, for example, once or twice weekly, may be considered as trading.

The exemption applies to a wide range of events, including quizzes, dances, concerts, fêtes and jumble sales.

The VAT exemption is mandatory for events that fulfil all the conditions and all the charity's income in connection with the event will be exempt, although the sale of commemorative goods for a period after the event will not enjoy VAT exemption. Goods and services purchased for the event are subject to the normal VAT treatment. However charities can make zero rated supplies at an event, for example through the sale of programmes and donated goods, and can claim back their input tax in relation to those supplies.

> **CAUTION!**
>
> If charities exceed the 15 event limit, none of the fundraising events will qualify for the VAT exemption.
>
> Charities can hold joint fundraising events with other charities, but be careful when holding joint events in partnership with non-charities as the exemption may not apply.

### VAT and branches

Where branches are part of the parent charity, the obligation to register for VAT is determined by the total taxable supplies of the branches and main charity combined. Where the branch is independent and legally separate from the parent, the requirement for the branch to register will be dependent on its own turnover of taxable supplies. In this situation, any donation made by the branch to the parent body which is a genuine donation (i.e. not a subscription for services) will be treated as non-business.

## Employment

As has been stated in chapter 6, when we discussed employment issues, charities must pay employers' national insurance contributions for all employees with an income above a certain level. Thresholds are reviewed annually so trustees are advised to check the current level, but in recent years, employer's national insurance contributions have been payable on salaries above the £4,500 mark, at a rate of around 12–13%.

Charity staff are, of course, required to pay income tax on their income and to pay national insurance contributions. A charity which operates its own payroll will be responsible for collecting these sums and passing payment to the government.

## Trading

There is a general presumption against commercial trading by charities. Charities are established to promote a particular charitable purpose and to act in the public interest and this is not always compatible with commercial trading. Depending on the wording of an individual charity's governing document, trading may be beyond the organisation's constitutional remit, so trustees who sanction such activities will be acting in breach of trust. In addition, commercial trading is financially risky and it is not appropriate for organisations to subject charitable funds to business risk. Finally, charities enjoy tax exemptions that are not available to commercial organisations so it would be inequitable for charities to compete with companies within the same arena. However the law is pragmatic: it recognises that there are occasions when charitable organisations will be perfectly justified in selling goods and services in order to meet charitable objectives and to raise funds, so some trading is permissible and exempt from tax, provided it falls within one of the following categories.

1   *Primary purpose trading.* This involves the sale of goods or services that fall directly within the primary objects of the charity. Such trading is permissible as it will further the objects of the charity. Ancillary trading, related to the primary purpose, is also acceptable.

**EXAMPLE**

A charity whose object is to promote the welfare of older people may charge for the provision of day centres, residential or domiciliary care. It is under this provision that many local charities are able to have service level agreements or other forms of contracts with statutory agencies for the provision of care services. Ancillary trading may include the sale of refreshments or emergency groceries in the day centre.

A charity with objects that include increasing the independence of people with disabilities may sell aids and adaptations.

Trading that is not wholly focussed on the charity's primary purpose will be acceptable provided the non-primary purpose element is small both in financial value and as a proportion of the trade as a whole.

2   *Small trading.* Charities can trade on a small scale outside their primary purpose. Small trading is restricted to a limited annual turnover of £5,000 or, if greater than £5,000, 25 per cent of the charity's annual income, subject to a maximum of £50,000. It may be acceptable for charities to exceed these limits if they had a

reasonable expectation that their turnover would be within the restrictions. Fundraising events may also be covered by the fundraising exemption (see the earlier discussion in the VAT section).

**EXAMPLE**

Charities may sell books or provide training not related to their primary purpose.

3 *Trade carried out by the beneficiaries.* Charities can trade in goods that have been manufactured by their beneficiaries and in services provided by the beneficiaries. The involvement of non-beneficiaries in the trade (for example in a management or advisory capacity) will not present problems as long as the majority of the work is carried out by beneficiaries.

**EXAMPLE**

Charity shops selling craft and art work produced by beneficiaries within a charity's sheltered workshop or a catering service staffed by people with learning disabilities.

Further tax exemptions are available for:
- the sale of donated goods, provided the goods have not been significantly modified; and
- profits from lettings where the income is used for charitable purposes (this exemption may be waived if additional services are provided).

Business sponsorship and payment for the use of a charity's logo may or may not be considered to be a trade and subject to tax, depending on the exact circumstances of the agreement between the parties. In addition, VAT may be payable.

**CAUTION!**

Even tax exempt trading may be subject to VAT. See the VAT section above for further information.

Charities which trade outside these permitted areas may find that they have acted outside the terms of their governing document and, consequently, the trustees have acted either ultra vires and/or in breach of trust. They may also find that they are required to pay tax on any profits from trading. It may be held to be inappropriate to claim these liabilities from charitable funds and that the trustees should pay.

Any profits from trading activities that are not covered by the tax exemptions will be subject to tax. When calculating profits, trustees should pay attention to any indirect overheads, such as accommodation of the trading activity within the charity's premises. Where goods or services have been supplied to the trading activity free of charge or at a reduced rate, trustees should consider the commercial value of such items when determining profits.

## Trading companies

There is a way for charities to trade outside of the permitted areas that does not expose charitable funds to business risk and does not result in a breach of trust. Charities wishing to trade on a larger scale may set up a separate trading company. This device may be used by charities wanting to trade outside of their primary objects and the tax concessions (e.g. for larger fundraising purposes) and by those who intend to trade within their objects but wish to protect the charity itself from the inherent business risks.

Trading companies operate as normal commercial companies, unrestricted by the limitations on charity trading. They may seek investment from a number of sources but are often established by charities as a wholly owned subsidiary, i.e. the charity is the sole shareholder, although this is not essential. Trading subsidiaries are subject to the same taxes as regular commercial companies. Under the gift aid scheme they may donate their profits, prior to the deduction of taxes, to the charity. The charity does not need to reclaim any tax and the company will receive a deduction in corporation tax in respect of the gift aid payment. The scheme allows for gift aid payments relating to a particular accounting period to be made up to nine months after the end of that accounting period.

The company will probably need to keep a proportion of its profits in order to maintain adequate cash balances to continue trading.

Alternatively the charity can establish the company with sufficient capital to allow it to gift all of its profits to the charity. However to qualify for the tax benefits, the charity's financial investment in setting up and maintaining the company must be made for charitable purposes only and for the benefit of the charity. It should also be secure and offer a fair rate of return, with provision for the recovery of any loans to the company. In addition, trustees should be aware that whilst trading losses on primary purpose trading may be classed as charitable expenditure, trading losses on non-primary purpose trading will be non-charitable expenditure and potentially ultra vires.

On a practical level, a number of the trustees of the charity should serve as directors of the subsidiary trading company in order to ensure that the company is operating in the interests of the charity, including consistency between the charity and the company in areas such as public image, employment practices etc. It is also advisable to bring in directors from the commercial sector who have appropriate business skills.

---

**WHEN TO SET UP A TRADING COMPANY**

**1** Do you want to trade on a regular, significant basis (i.e. not small trading)?
*No – trading company not necessary*
*Yes – go to 2*

**2** Do you want to trade outside the primary objects of the charity or enter into trading that is not carried out by your beneficiaries?
*No – trading company not necessary, go to 3*
*Yes – trading company necessary*

**3** Is the level of trading or the capital investment required such that it is necessary to protect the charity from business risks?
*No – trading company not required*
*Yes – trading company necessary*

---

**PROPOSED CHANGES – TRADING**

Following its review of charity law, the Cabinet Office Strategy Unit has recommended that charities should be able to undertake all trading within the charity without the need for a separate trading company.

Implementation of this proposal would require legislative change.

## Developing an investment policy

Trustees have an obligation to maximise the funds available for furthering the objects of the charity. For many charities this means fundraising to support a hand-to-mouth existence, but for those organisations that hold reserves or endowments, the obligation extends to the investment of those funds.

Whether the charity is holding the next quarter's grant cheque or a permanent endowment, decisions need to be made about where best to place the funds to maximise the resources available to develop the charity's work. For this, charities need an investment policy and trustees need, as a starting point, to have agreed the direction of the charity and determined the resources necessary to reach that destination. There are two key questions on which an investment policy rests:

1  capital or income?
2  long term or short term?

Does the charity need to accrue capital, e.g. for the purchase or refurbishment of a building or to update equipment or does it need its investments to bring in a regular income to fund the charity's work? Does it need the money in the short term (e.g. to fund a individual piece of work) or is it a medium or long-term requirement, perhaps to fund expansion or to make up the shortfall of a predicted loss of income, such as the end of a fixed-term grant? Few cases will be black and white, with many investment policies involving a mixed approach of capital and income returns and long and short-term investments. The function of the trustees is to determine the balance between the different demands.

Is quick access to the funds likely to be needed? How much of your balance can be committed to investments on a long-term basis and how much should be kept in more open investments that will allow funds to be withdrawn swiftly in the event of an emergency? For example, trustees may decide to keep the equivalent of one month's running costs or an adequate sum for emergency building repairs in a more flexible investment.

### Balance of risk

Trustees also need to consider the level of risk into which they are prepared to enter and this should be included within the policy.

Unfortunately, the nature of the investment market means that the highest returning investments carry the highest risks and those that are lowest risk offer less return. There are limits on the investment opportunities available to charities precisely because it would be inappropriate for trustees to place charitable funds in highly risky investments. Restrictions on charity investment are considered in more detail in the next sections. Within the investments that are available, trustees must decide how they wish to balance risk against returns.

### Ethical investment

Investment decisions can be difficult for those with a social conscience. Many charity trustees may be understandably reluctant to invest charitable funds in companies or governments the activities of which the trustees consider to be morally questionable. However, trustees need to balance any qualms against their obligation to act in the best interests of the charity and to maximise the resources available. This is not a straightforward equation. Even a high returning investment can damage a charity's funding base if the investment in question directly contradicts the organisation's objects or is so unpopular with donors that it results in a loss of fundraising income. As a result, some basic principles have evolved.

1 Charities should not make investments that contradict the objects of the charity as these would not further the charity's objects and as such may result in a breach of trust (because the trustees have acted outside the objects).

**EXAMPLES**

Charities involved in cancer research and treatment should not invest in tobacco companies and charities supporting landmine victims should not invest in arms companies. Similarly, charities supporting refugees who are seeking asylum from particular regimes should not buy the government bonds of those regimes.

2 Charities may decide not to make investments that they reasonably believe would adversely affect fundraising income.

**EXAMPLE**

A charity working with older people might decide not to invest in cosmetic companies that test products on animals, provided that it could establish that this would deter donors from making further gifts, e.g. because of the weight of public opinion against such testing or because of the expressed opinions of the charity's regular donors.

3   Trustees cannot, however, decide not to purchase a particular investment simply because it would be against personal conscience. Some potential adverse affect on the charity must be demonstrated.

**EXAMPLE**

Trustees of a disability charity could not make a decision not to invest in a fast food company simply because they personally advocated healthy eating and were consequently opposed to fast food.

Ethical investment questions focus very much on screening out inappropriate investments and, as such, this is sometimes seen as a negative approach. The alternative, known as socially responsible investment, aims to proactively invest in those companies with good track records in chosen areas, such as employment practice, environmental responsibility and corporate social involvement.

The investment policy is an important tool for trustees to instruct and monitor their advisers. As well as shaping the requirements of the investments in terms of the nature of the return, balance of risk and any ethical

**PROPOSED CHANGES – ETHICAL INVESTMENT**

The Cabinet Office Strategy Unit has recommended that, given that returns on ethical funds are similar to non-ethical funds, the ability of charities to adopt a broad ethical policy should be clarified. It also proposes that charities with an annual income of over £1m should be required to declare their position on ethical investment within their annual reports (this would require legislative change) and that smaller charities should declare their position as a matter of good practice.

restrictions, the policy should also consider the charity's investment powers and any restrictions on investments, as determined by the organisation's governing document and by law.

## Investments

### The law and the governing document

Trustees have a general power of investment. This was introduced by the Trustee Act 2000 and supersedes the limited powers that existed under previous legislation, even where these are specifically mentioned in a charity's governing document. Within this general power, existing restrictions or exclusions on specific types of investment that may be included in the governing document (e.g. a restriction on the purchase of shares in tobacco companies) are still valid. If trustees wish to remove these restrictions, they should consult the Charity Commission.

The general power of investment allows for trustees to place charity funds in any kind of investment (except land) as if they were the absolute owner of those funds. However, trustees are required to seek appropriate advice and to consider the suitability of investments and the need to diversify the range of investments held. They are also required to review their investments.

Trustees can delegate investment functions but any delegated asset management must be under a written agreement and must be reviewed periodically.

### Different types of investments

There is a large range of investments available for charities to choose from and the terminology can be bewildering for the uninitiated.

*Shares* are sold by companies to raise revenue. There is no obligation for companies to repay, or buy back shares. The owners of the shares (the shareholders) share in the ownership and profits of the company. Profits are distributed through dividends. There are different types of shares and this affects the dividend received:

1 Owners of ordinary shares (also known as equities) may not receive a dividend if the company is in financial trouble, but will receive higher dividends in successful years. Ordinary shareholders also have voting rights at general meetings.

2 Preference shares pay a predetermined dividend, unconnected to the company's profit level. Although preference shareholders take priority over ordinary shareholders in the payment of dividends, they have limited voting rights.

3 Debentures pay a specified dividend at specified intervals.

4 Convertible shares pay a fixed rate of interest, rather than a dividend, but may be converted into ordinary shares at some point in the future.

*Bonds* are also sold to raise revenue but do not confer any ownership or pay out profits. Instead, bonds pay a fixed rate of interest (the coupon) to the bond holder up to the set date when the issuer of the bond will repay the holder. This is called the redemption or maturity date. They may be issued by companies (corporate bonds) and by statutory bodies, including overseas governments. UK government bonds are known as gilts. Interest rates tend to be lower on the more secure bonds, e.g. gilts, and higher on the riskier investments, such as corporate bonds. Bonds are also known as fixed interest stocks or fixed interest securities.

*Stock* is the overall term for shares, bonds and gilts. Stock may be bought and sold freely, hence the term 'stock market'.

*Deposits* are funds kept with financial institutions such as banks and building societies. The rate of interest paid on deposits is variable. Accounts that offer access to funds with little or no notice often have low interest rates, whereas those with long notice periods offer higher interest, with penalties on early withdrawal.

*Property* can also be an investment. Property is dealt with separately, later in this chapter.

*Yield* is the annual return received from an investment, e.g. in dividends or interest.

*Collective investments* provide opportunities to invest relatively small sums of money in the stock market whilst spreading those funds across a wide range of stock. The basic premise is that the resources of a group of investors are collectively invested and managed for the common benefit, with the yield from the investments distributed amongst the different investors. There are a number of different forms of collective investments.

1 Unit trusts – here, the total investment is divided into units. The individual units represent a proportion of the value of all the investments held and income received from the investment is distributed

to unit holders in accordance with the number of units held. Alternatively income may be accumulated for the benefit of the unit holders. Investments are selected according to the objectives of the particular scheme, i.e. capital or income. Management fees are charged and some unit trusts charge exit fees. Returns are not guaranteed.

2 Investment trusts are companies which invest in shares. Investors buy shares in the investment trust company itself, with the company issuing a fixed number of shares. Share price is determined by a number of factors, including the value of the investments in the fund and supply and demand. Charges include the dealing price of buying and selling the shares.

3 Open ended investment companies (OEICs) manage investment funds and you invest in them by purchasing shares. Unlike investment trusts, OEICs can continue to issue shares in response to demand. There may be an initial charge for share purchase or an exit charge for leaving the OEIC.

4 A common investment fund is a form of collective investment that is only available to registered charities. These are themselves registered charities and work on a similar model to unit trusts; however charges are lower with a smaller minimum investment.

Those who invest in these collective vehicles are not the owners of the shares, instead shares are owned by the fund, company or trust.

When reviewing the investment opportunities available, in partnership with their professional advisers, trustees should consider the requirements of their investment policy. For example, cash and bonds are low-risk investments but may not offer sufficient returns to protect against inflation. In contrast, equities tend to offer long-term protection against inflation but charities will need to balance their selection of shares against their accepted risk level and any ethical concerns. Other issues to consider will be the need to access funds (as has already been said, some high interest bearing deposits have lengthy notice periods) and whether the charges made in relation to certain investments are justified by the level of return. The likely response will be a diversified approach, with investments spread across cash deposits, shares and bonds. This offers a trade off between risk and return. However the balance of this spread will depend on the policy of the charity.

## Professional advisers

Once you have developed your investment policy, it is time to call in the professionals. The investment market is complex and subject to frequent fluctuations and few trustees will be truly qualified to manage charities' investments in a detailed way. Most charities will need to place funds in a variety of different investments in order to meet the requirements of their investment policy by achieving the desired balance of income and capital generation, long and short-term investments and also catering for risk and ethical considerations. This range of investments is known as an investment portfolio and the management of this portfolio is the responsibility of a fund or investment manager. The fund manager will normally be employed by an investment company and is the professional appointed by the trustees to make detailed decisions about when to switch funds between different investments, perhaps to reduce risk or increase returns, whilst maintaining the balance and generating the returns required by the charity's investment policy. Alternatively, an investment broker may serve as an intermediary between the board and the fund manager.

### Appointing a fund manager

Some investment companies do specialise in working with medium sized charities, but trustees may have to shop around for these services. It is worth considering the service provided by a number of different companies, paying particular attention to the points listed below.

*Authorisation.* Check that the fund manager is authorised to carry out investment business by the Financial Services Authority (see further pp. 182–183).

*Charges.* Fund managers' fees will depend on the service offered and the size of your investments. Charges may be expressed as a percentage of the portfolio value based on a sliding scale (the larger the investment, the smaller the percentage fee) or on the number of transactions. Look out for any hidden fees, e.g. for producing reports.

*Services.* The different services available include discretionary management (where the fund manager makes the decisions) and advisory services (where the manager always consults the client before making transactions). Consider whether investments are made in tracker funds (i.e. money is invested in a set group of companies) or actively managed;

whether cash management services are available (if required); and whether any ethical concerns can be accommodated.

*Past performance.* Although not always an indicator of future success, trustees should look for a consistent track record in terms of investment performance and also question the company's stability, particularly in terms of retaining key staff.

*Personality.* Trustees need to be comfortable that their fund manager is someone whom they respect and feel confident working with.

*Voting.* You may want to consider the investment company's approach to shareholder voting. Does it exercise its right to vote and, if so, does it consult its clients (who are the beneficial shareholders) on the direction of the voting?

*Other issues.* Trustees may also want to consider a range of other issues, such as the company's risk management strategy, internal controls, arrangements for reporting to clients and charity experience.

Once appropriate firms have been identified, ask them to submit written proposals in response to the charity's investment policy and shortlist a number of firms to meet with before making the final decision.

## Monitoring the fund manager's performance

Trustees should monitor fund managers' performance against an agreed standard or benchmark. This may be negotiated with the fund manager, based on the expectations of the investment policy, it may be linked to a particular stock market index or it may be a published common benchmark (known as a 'universe'), based on the opinions of a range of industry specialists

Charities should keep all correspondence and documentation regarding the relationship with the fund manager.

The appointment of the fund manager should also be subject to regular review, e.g. every three years, in order to ensure that the chosen fund manager remains the most appropriate for the charity. If at any point the trustees have serious concerns about the appointment, it should be reviewed immediately.

## Protection for investors

All investment managers must be authorised under the Financial Services and Markets Act 2000 and regulated by the Financial Services Authority

(FSA). The FSA is the investment industry regulator and keeps a register of the firms that are authorised to conduct investment business. In order to be placed on the FSA's register firms must meet certain requirements in relation to competence, financial stability and treatment of customers. The register includes the details of the services that each firm is authorised to deliver and details of any disciplinary action that has been taken against the firm. Investors can access the FSA's register through the FSA's Firm Check Service.

In the event of a complaint regarding an investment professional, trustees should first contact the firm in question (details of whom to contact within the firm are available on the FSA's register). If their response is not satisfactory, the issue may be raised with the FSA. If an authorised firm has been used, access to complaints procedures and compensation is provided through the Financial Ombudsman Service and the Financial Services Compensation Scheme. (See the Directory for contact details.)

## Appointing nominees and custodians

Trustees involved in the management of investments or land may find that a nominee or custodian is required.

- *Nominee.* A nominee is appointed by the trustees to hold the charity's property. The property, e.g. shares, is held in the name of the nominee but on behalf of the charity.
- *Custodian.* Custodians have custody of a charity's assets, or documents relating to those assets, for safe-keeping.

Nominee and custodial services can be particularly useful if the charity has extensive documentation in relation to its assets or has a frequent turnover of trustees, as these services prevent the need for repeated legal transfers of property or handing over of documentation.

Charities have a statutory power to appoint nominees and custodians, unless this is specifically excluded by the governing document. The power does not apply to assets which are vested in the Official Custodian for Charities (see the section on property and land below) or where the charity has its own custodian trustee, as is often the case with older, land owning charities. There must be written evidence of the appointment and the individual or organisation appointed must be appropriate.

Trustees may determine the conditions of appointment, including remuneration, bearing in mind the requirements of the governing document and the need to avoid conflicts of interest. The appointment should be reviewed periodically. Trustees must ensure that the charity's ownership of the assets in question remains legally provable and should receive reports from the nominee or custodian regarding the arrangements to ensure safe keeping of the charity's property.

## INVESTMENT CHECKLIST

- ☑ Are your investments allowed by law and your governing document?
- ☑ Is the balance right between capital and income returns?
- ☑ Is the balance right between short, medium and long-term returns?
- ☑ Is the level of risk appropriate for your organisation?
- ☑ Do the investments comply with your requirements regarding ethical issues?
- ☑ Is your fund manager authorised by the Financial Services Authority?
- ☑ Is your fund manager operating within your investment strategy?
- ☑ Is your fund manager supplying adequate and useful information?
- ☑ Is the performance of your fund manager meeting your requirements?
- ☑ Are you reviewing your investments regularly?

## Property and land

### GENERAL PRINCIPLES

Charities must always engage appropriate professional support, including solicitors and surveyors, when considering land transactions. Provisions are complex and the discussion below can only give an overview of some of the key requirements.

Land transactions must be in the best interests of the charity, which means securing the best price, best mortgage deals etc.

Land transactions between the charity and a connected party (e.g. a trustee) represent a conflict of interest and should be discussed with the Charity Commission.

Trustees should seek advice on proposed land transactions involving permanent endowments.

## Authority to own land

There is a general statutory power for charities to acquire land in the UK for charitable or investment purposes. Charities with governing documents that expressly contradict this power should check with the Charity Commission before purchasing land. Trustees should engage professional advice as necessary and ensure that the purchase is in the best interests of the charity, e.g. the property should be appropriate for its intended use, with any necessary planning permission in place, the price (and mortgage terms) should be fair, and the charity should be able to afford the purchase and any corresponding mortgage.

If purchasing the property for investment purposes, the general investment provisions apply, i.e. the trustees must seek appropriate professional advice and the investment must be suitable and part of a diversified range of investments. As with other investments, the investment in property should be subject to review. Trustees should pay particular attention to the need to actively manage property investments and the difficulty in withdrawing funds from such investments.

Mortgages and charities are not a natural partnership and restrictions do apply. A charity wishing to take out a mortgage on new or existing property should have appropriate powers within its governing document (if not, it should contact the Charity Commission). The trustees should also seek appropriate advice on the need for the loan, the suitability of the terms of the loan and their ability to repay it.

## Disposal of charity land

Many governing documents give trustees the power to dispose of charity land and this is supported by a general statutory power. Constitutional powers may be subject to certain conditions, such as public notice of disposal of property that is central to the charity's objects (e.g. a playground or village hall). Any such conditions should be followed. There are similar statutory provisions in place requiring charities to give public notice of the intention to dispose of land that is held for a specific purpose.

In order to reduce the risk of conflicts of interest and fraud, any decisions or actions in relation to the disposal or mortgaging of charity land must be taken by the trustees acting together and should not be delegated to a single trustee, employee or adviser.

Charities leasing their land to another party should seek legal advice in drawing up the terms of the tenancy agreement.

## Documentation

As discussed above, trustees may decide to pass property documentation (title deeds, land registry certificates etc.) to a custodian. Any custodian trustee (including the Official Custodian of Charities) must be party to the transfer of charity property.

Although trustees must act collectively when disposing of land, only two trustees need to sign the deeds.

Trustees who dispose of charity land are required to include certain statements and certificates in the contract with the purchaser and in the conveyance, lease, transfer and any other deed or document affecting the disposal. Similar requirements are in place for mortgage deeds. There are prescribed forms of these statements and certificates in relation to registered land. In other cases, the solicitor will determine the wording. The purpose of this requirement is to ensure that the purchaser is aware that the land has been bought from a charity and to enable trustees to certify that they have followed the relevant requirements.

## Official Custodian for Charities

The Official Custodian for Charities holds land, and very occasionally investments, on behalf of charities. The Official Custodian is an employee of the Charity Commission. As with other custodian services, this means that there is no need to make new deeds in relation to the property when the trustees change. It eliminates the risk of charity property being vested in individuals who have since moved on and are no longer connected with the organisation. If this does happen, vesting the land in the Official Custodian is a means of demonstrating the charity's ownership.

Property is vested in the Official Custodian by an order of the court or of the Charity Commissioners. Charities can apply for an order of the Commissioners and appropriate forms are available from the Commission. The services of the Official Custodian are free of charge.

The Official Custodian does not become involved in managing the property: this responsibility remains with the trustees. The trustees normally retain the title deeds and related documentation.

## Maintenance and health and safety requirements

Charities that own land will be responsible for the maintenance of that land, insurance arrangements and compliance with any related health and safety requirements, unless the land is leased to a third party in which case responsibility will be determined by the tenancy agreement. Trustees should pay full attention to their obligations in this respect (see chapter 2).

# **9** Fundraising

## INTRODUCTION

Some organisations, such as grant-making trusts with extensive endowments, are in the fortunate position of not having to raise funds to survive, but for most charities fundraising is crucial to their ongoing viability. Although some charities survive solely on goodwill and voluntary effort, the majority reach a point at which cash is essential to sustain the organisation and give future stability. As trustees are responsible for the financial health of their charity, they must ensure that it has adequate resources to deliver its objectives. However trustees' responsibility for fundraising extends beyond the bottom line, as there are also areas of concern regarding regulation, public relations issues and delegated activities within the organisation.

In this chapter we will be looking at trustees' responsibilities in relation to fundraising, including developing the strategy and ensuring that fundraising activities stay within the law. However, this will not include advice on how to raise money or advice on different fundraising approaches. There are many books on the practical aspects of fundraising and a selection is listed in the Directory.

## Developing the fundraising strategy

Fundraising should be an integral part of the trustees' planning process. In earlier chapters we have looked at trustees' roles in relation to business planning, budget setting and investment. As part of these processes trustees must determine how much money they need to run existing services and to establish new ones. Within this global figure, the different sources of income should be identified and this information will form the foundation of the fundraising strategy. In this section, we will consider the areas to cover when developing a fundraising strategy. An action plan that can be used to draft your strategy is included at the end of this section.

## Where is the money coming from?

Relying on a single source of income makes an organisation extremely insecure should that source of income cease. For example, historically many local charities have been largely or entirely financed by local authority grants and so have been highly vulnerable to funding cuts. Diversifying income sources offers charities a degree of protection, or at least some breathing space, should an income stream run dry. Different areas of work may lend themselves naturally to certain sources of income and some income streams may already be secure. For example, charities may already have a number of service level agreements or grants in place. Additional revenue projects, such as the appointment of a worker dedicated to supporting a particular element of the client group, are probably best funded by renewable grants or service level agreements. In contrast, one-off grants, donations and investment income may appropriately fund a capital project, e.g. a building extension, or a time-limited revenue project, such as a pilot study. Fundraising events and street collections can be useful ways of raising funds that can be used for any purpose within the organisation.

Any ethical issues relating to sources of funds should be considered, and this may be linked into the charity's ethical investment policy. If the charity would not invest in tobacco companies, should it accept donations from them? Trustees may agree on wider restrictions, for example not to raise money through gambling or not to seek lottery grants. As always with ethical issues, trustees should ensure that any self-imposed restrictions on sources of fundraising income are in the best interests of the charity, either because of the risk of direct conflict with charitable objects or because of a likely negative impact on other funding streams.

Trustees may want to divide their fundraising strategy into fundraising for restricted funds (money given for a specific purpose that cannot be applied to any other activity within the organisation) and unrestricted funds (i.e. money that can be applied as the charity wishes within its overall purposes). More information on restricted and unrestricted funds is given in chapter 7. Many charities find it easier to raise restricted funds, as corporate sponsors, grant makers and the public like to feel that they are supporting a specific piece of work. Unrestricted funds to finance the general activities and overheads of the charity may be raised through a variety of approaches, including general appeals, fundraising events, trading income and legacies.

## Timescale

As well as identifying the amount and sources of income, the fundraising strategy should look at the funding timescale. It is no good raising money in two years' time for a project that is currently only funded for the next six months. By identifying what money is needed and when, trustees can prioritise the different elements of the strategy and create an action plan. In this way, the fundraising strategy will be closely linked to the business plan.

Timescales should also be set for each appeal, indicating when the appeal will end. This makes for better appeal planning and facilitates clearer accounting of appeal funds.

## 'Joined up thinking'

As well as linking into business planning, budgeting and the investment policy, the fundraising strategy should be consistent with any public relations approach agreed by the organisation, be complementary to operational work, and be sympathetic with the organisation's objectives. It may be considered inappropriate for an charity working to alleviate family poverty to raise funds through events involving gambling, such as a race night. Similarly an charity promoting the independence of its beneficiaries would have its message undermined by a fundraising campaign that evoked a pity from the public. Furthermore aggressive fundraising campaigns, for example high profile street collections, telephone fundraising and seeking to sign up direct debit donors on local high streets, can lead to public resentment and be counter productive in terms of public relations.

## Is it worth it?

The strategy should also consider the 'effort:reward' equation. Will the anticipated income justify the amount of effort (and any money) invested in raising the funds? Small efforts can reap great rewards. In contrast there have been cases where huge fundraising campaigns or high salaries paid to specialist fundraising staff have not managed to generate enough extra income to break even. For local charities, fundraising events can be a labour intensive option but may only generate small financial rewards, although the collateral benefits of increased profile or user involvement may make such events worthwhile.

As part of the fundraising strategy, consider the investment of time or money in each fundraising approach alongside the anticipated outcome. The reward should always be greater than the effort, although it is for the trustees to decide in each case whether the reward is sufficient to make the effort worthwhile. For example is expenditure of £1,000 generating a total income of £1,500 and a net gain of £500 justifiable or would the activity have to generate a net income of £1,000 to be worthwhile?

The trustees should also question whether the anticipated outcome is a realistic prediction. Are estimated returns for a street collection, legacy appeal or other fundraising event based on guesswork, previous experience or some other calculation? Are grant applications likely to be successful – for example, have the applications been targeted at those grant makers most likely to fund your type of organisation or project?

## Reporting the costs

The amount of money spent on fundraising should be reported in the charity's annual accounts. Some fundraising activities also serve as a means of promoting charitable objectives, e.g. if they raise awareness of the charity's work. There is a degree of latitude in the way that trustees can apportion costs between the promotion of charitable objects and fundraising expenses.

## Who is responsible?

Are trustees or staff responsible for fundraising? This question should be considered as part of the fundraising strategy and reflected in the job descriptions of staff. Fundraising is one of those areas of charity work that can easily fall through the gaps in clearly defined responsibilities of staff and trustees, particularly in small charities.

Trustees should be clear about who will take responsibility for the day-to-day tasks involved in fundraising, from rattling a tin through to negotiating with grant making bodies. If these tasks are to be delegated to a member of staff, the scope of the role should be explicitly described in the employee's job description and the skills and experience required should be an integral part of the person specification. As always, trustees

**CASE EXAMPLE**

A local charity providing social welfare services was financed by fixed-term funding from the local authority. The grant paid the salaries of a support worker and a part-time administrator. The organisation had no other paid staff. The support worker focussed on delivering the charity's objectives by providing services to clients and expected the trustees to secure continuing funding; however, the trustees expected the worker to negotiate with the local authority for a new grant. Responsibility for securing income had not been defined, with the result that the worker took extended sick leave due to stress caused by the competing demands on her time, lack of clarity regarding her role, and job insecurity, due to the uncertain funding situation.

should be conscious of the blend of skills that they are looking for and the balance between fundraising and other activities. In the case study above, it was unrealistic of the trustees to expect a worker who had been employed for social care and counselling skills also to be an experienced fundraiser. It was also unrealistic to expect the worker to take a lead role in securing ongoing funding without compromising an already full workload of client services. In these circumstances, the trustees had a clear responsibility to seek ongoing funding in order to sustain the charity and they should have taken the lead in the negotiations with the local authority.

Trustees of small charities should be particularly wary of asking their staff to fundraise where the income generated will be used to pay the salaries of those staff. This gives the appearance that the staff are acting in their own interests and some grant-making bodies will not consider applications that are presented on this basis unless the trustees also have an active input into the application process.

In charities with a staff team, it may be more appropriate for trustees to delegate fundraising activities amongst the staff, particularly if the team includes employees dedicated to the internal functioning and development of the organisation rather than operational roles. For example, a chief executive, office manager or finance manager may all play active roles in fundraising, from drafting funding applications through to arranging street collections or fundraising events.

## Fundraising strategy – action plan

| Task | Who is responsible? |
| --- | --- |
| Identify short, medium and long-term fundraising targets. | Trustees, with the support of any finance and fundraising staff and the chief officer. |
| Identify the most appropriate sources of funding. | Trustees and senior staff, including any fundraising staff. |
| Check that the proposed fundraising approach is consistent with the organisation's public image and operational concerns. | Trustees and senior staff, in consultation with operational staff and any PR personnel. |
| Agree a baseline in terms of the ratio of fundraising costs to fundraising income. | Trustees (particularly the treasurer), senior officer and senior finance officer. |
| Agree how fundraising costs will be reported in the accounts. | Trustees (particularly the treasurer), senior officer and senior finance officer. |
| Allocate resources (people and budget) to fundraising work. Include the contributions of volunteers. Check human resources allocation is appropriate given staff skills and workload. | Trustees and senior staff. |
| Consider any legal restrictions or best practice issues relating to your preferred methods of fundraising. | Trustees with the advice and support of senior staff. |

Larger organisations, particularly national charities or those with large overheads (e.g. residential and educational facilities), often employ dedicated fundraising staff to bring in the required revenue. Trustees continue to have the ultimate responsibility for the financial viability of the organisation and the appointment of professional fundraising staff does not absolve them of this responsibility: it merely allows them to delegate the fundraising task to people with appropriate skills and experience. In the worst case scenario, if the organisation fails and does not have adequate funds to make redundancy payments to staff and meet its obligations to other creditors, it is the trustees who will be sued.

The fundraising of many local charities is led by volunteers. Whilst such volunteers are often extremely successful and hugely valuable to the charity, trustees must retain responsibility for fundraising and exercise authority over the actions of volunteers. This is frequently achieved through a fundraising sub-committee involving trustees and volunteers.

The use of fundraising consultants is discussed at pp. 200–203.

## Rules and good practice

Trustees also need to be aware of the regulatory framework that surrounds fundraising activities. In addition to the information given below, the application of other legal requirements should also be considered. For example, information held on donors is subject to the provisions of the Data Protection Act 1998 and health and safety requirements should be complied with in relation to any fundraising events. Both of these subjects are discussed in chapter 2.

The focus of this section is on those fundraising activities that are most commonly used by small to medium-sized charities. Activities that are primarily used by large charities, e.g. overseas challenge events and internet fundraising, are not discussed here. Sources of information on these activities are listed in the Directory.

### Street collections

A permit or licence is normally required for charity collections or sales taking place in the street or other public places. Licences and permits can be obtained from the relevant local authority or, for collections in London, from the police or the City of London.

Permits and licences are granted under local regulations. Issues that will be considered include obstructions to both human and vehicular traffic, financial controls and accounting arrangements for any funds raised through the collection, and the frequency of collections (some high streets have street collections booked throughout the year, whilst other local authorities prefer to keep the number of collections down). Contact your local authority for information about the regulations in your area. Pay particular attention to arrangements for public places that are privately owned, e.g. shopping centres and railway stations.

## Door-to-door collections

Door-to-door, or house-to-house, collections are also subject to licensing arrangements, again controlled by the local authority or, in London, the police or the City of London. The arrangements apply to charity sales and collections of money and goods from residential and business premises (including public houses). Exemptions from the licensing requirement are available from the Home Secretary for collections covering a wide area (i.e. a substantial part of the country). Exemptions are available from the police for local collections taking place over a short period of time.

---

**tip**

It is good practice to collect cash donations from street and door-to-door collections in sealed collecting tins. This not only helps reduce the risk of theft from the collection, but also reassures donors that the risk of theft has been reduced.

Those collecting public donations should always wear visible identity cards establishing their connection with the charity and the legality of the collection.

---

**PROPOSED CHANGES – LICENSING FOR PUBLIC COLLECTIONS**

As a result of its review of charity law, the Cabinet Office Strategy Unit has proposed that there should be a new unified local authority licensing scheme for public collections.

---

## Events

Charities raise funds through a wide variety of events, from jumble sales and raffles through to high profile auctions and expensive balls. Trustees need to research carefully any legal requirements relating to the events planned. The tax exemptions available for fundraising and trading are discussed in chapter 8. Other issues include health and safety requirements (e.g. maximum capacity for venues used), insurance and specific regulations relating to the nature of the event, such as any licences required for gambling or the sale of alcohol.

## Lotteries (including raffles)

Charities and their subsidiary companies may run lotteries to raise money for their charitable purposes. Charity lotteries fall into two categories.

1 *Small lotteries.* There is no requirement to register a small lottery, but they must comply with certain conditions and be incidental to an exempt entertainment, for example fêtes and concerts (for more information see the tax exemptions for fundraising events discussed in chapter 8). The classic example of a small lottery is a raffle. Raffles generally comply with all the requirements, i.e. tickets must be sold and issued and the results announced during the event and on the premises where it is held, there can be no cash prizes and the maximum that can be spent on prizes is £250.

2 *Society lotteries.* Lotteries covering a wider audience must be registered with the local authority or the Gaming Board. Gaming Board registration is required where ticket sales exceed £20,000 for a single lottery or £250,000 for lotteries undertaken in a one-year period. Trustees undertaking society lotteries should contact their local authority or (if necessary) the Gaming Board for information on the detailed requirements relating to issues such as the price of tickets, prize money, deduction of costs, age restrictions and accounting requirements.

Trustees should also consult the Gaming Board if they wish to run competitions such as bingo or use slot machines for fundraising purposes.

Lottery profits are tax exempt as long as they are used solely for the charity's objects and all regulatory requirements are complied with. The tax exemption does not apply to lotteries run by subsidiary companies, although the company can donate all pre-tax profits to the charity under the gift aid scheme (see chapter 8).

## Telephone and broadcast media fund-raising

Codes of conduct are available for both telephone fundraising (Institute of Fundraising) and broadcast appeals (Broadcast Appeals Consortium). Even trustees of small charities may find opportunities for broadcast appeals, for example on local radio and television.

Trustees have a duty to ensure clarity in terms of identifying the charity (not just the cause) that will receive the funds and the proportion of the donation that will be spent on the charity's objects. Funds raised must be transferred directly to the charity.

## Legacies

Legacy fundraising is obviously a long-term fundraising approach and as such is probably best used by charities which have a sufficiently stable income to allow them to be confident that they will still be in existence when the legacy becomes available. It is also a sensitive and complex area of fundraising, and trustees looking to raise resources through legacies should plan their approach carefully. It is particularly important to develop a code for fundraisers, be they volunteers, employees or external fundraisers, that covers legal requirements and best practice. Such a code should also consider wider issues, such as the marketing of a legacy campaign. An insensitive campaign runs the risk of offending people and alienating potential donors. The Institute of Fundraising has produced a code of practice for legacy fundraising: see the Directory.

When seeking legacies, it is important to follow the basic principles of fundraising, including communicating clear information on the organisation's charitable status and the way in which the donation will be used. Given the sensitivity of legacy fundraising, it is critical that donors are not pressurised into making a donation. Particular care should be taken with dealing with vulnerable people, e.g. those who are terminally ill or recently bereaved. If it can be proved that the legacy was made under undue influence, the will could be held to be invalid and the gift will fail. It is clearly in the charity's best interests that wills are made with legal advice and fundraisers should recommend to donors that they consult an appropriate professional, although fundraisers should not recommend or comment on the competence of individual solicitors. In addition, wills must not be witnessed by a representative of the charity.

It is not unusual for donors to want their legacy to be used for a particular purpose. Charities must not accept legacies that are dependent upon conditions that they cannot fulfil or that would undermine their charitable status. Instead, fundraisers should communicate clearly to donors the extent to which their gifts can be dedicated to a particular project and seek to ensure that they understand how the funds will be used.

## Declaration of charitable status

Registered charities with a gross annual income of £10,000 or more are required to declare their charitable status on all media that solicits funds. It is good practice for all charities to do so. Similarly, although charities are not required to state their Charity Commission registration number, it is good practice to do so.

## Restricted funds

If funds have been raised for a particular purpose, they may only be spent on that purpose. This principle of restricted funds applies to public appeals as well as grant applications and can create difficulties if a specific fundraising appeal is more, or less, successful than anticipated. In such circumstances any unspent funds can not be applied to other causes within the charity without the express permission of the donor.

Many charities prefer to base fundraising campaigns and street collections on a specific issue, partly because they need money for that particular cause but also because, as has already been said, people like to give on this basis rather than just contributing to a general fund. If, as in the first example in the box below, more funds are raised than required, the charity will have to seek advice from the Charity Commission on

---

**CASE EXAMPLES**

A local youth charity needed new instruments for the youth club band. It raised money through a series of street collections, specifically requesting funds for instruments. The collection was extremely successful and after purchasing all the instruments that it could use and store, the charity had £1,000 left over from the collection. The trustees wanted to use this money to purchase new sports equipment, but were not able to do so as the donations had been given for instruments and as such were a restricted fund.

A village hall undertook a fundraising campaign to fund an extension to the hall. The appeal target was £100,000 but only half of that sum was raised. The £50,000 secured was not adequate to fund the building work but as the money had been raised for a specific purpose, the trustees of the hall could not apply it elsewhere.

---

whether a Commission Scheme will be necessary to enable the funds to be used for other purposes within the charity's objects. If the funds raised are insufficient, trustees must try to return any funds given by identifiable donors. If donors do not wish to take their money back, they must sign a disclaimer to this effect. Funds raised through collecting tins, competitions and lotteries are presumed to be from unidentifiable donors. The Charity Commission can make a Scheme to apply any remaining funds to other similar purposes within the charity. These funds must be kept in reserve for six months in order to meet any outstanding claims from donors.

Trustees facing either situation should contact the Commission for advice. However, this problem may be prevented altogether by leading a fundraising campaign with a specific appeal but stating that any funds raised that are not needed or cannot be used for that appeal will be applied to other work within the charity's objects. Such plans should be clearly stated in fundraising documentation.

## Audit trail

The handling of cash donations is an area where even well managed charities can come unstuck due to poor cash handling procedures. Organisations that receive cash donations or undertake any form of public collection should have clear financial procedures relating to the recording of cash receipts. Procedures should cover issues such as the use of sealed collecting tins and envelopes, joint counting of donated cash, and the provision of receipts to known donors.

Funds given for a specific appeal should be treated as restricted funds, subject to the discussion above, and so should be recorded as such on receipt.

## Institute of Fundraising: Donors' Charter and codes of fundraising practice

In response to public concerns about charity fundraising techniques, the Institute of Fundraising has developed a 'Donors' Charter' of good fundraising practice. The charter rests on some basic principles including:

- honesty, transparency and legal compliance by the charity;
- respect for the donor, including consideration of the donor's wishes, privacy, confidentiality and data protection concerns; and

- responsible handling of the donation, covering the use of the donation for the purposes given and for the greatest advantage of the beneficiaries, whilst preserving the dignity of beneficiaries.

The charter also covers arrangements for handling complaints made by donors.

The Institute has also developed a range of codes of practice for a number of fundraising activities. Copies of the charter and the codes of practice are available on the Institute's website (details can be found in the Directory).

### Unauthorised fund-raising

Unfortunately, some charities encounter problems with over-zealous supporters who raise funds on behalf of the charity without the organisation's consent. This may lead to regulatory problems, clashes with the charity's fundraising policy and alienation of the organisation's existing or potential supporters. Problems may also occur if a professional fundraiser with whom the charity has an agreement acts outside that agreement. Of course the first approach is for charities to seek to persuade the fundraiser to stop the unauthorised activity. However legal redress is also available in the form of an injunction to prevent unauthorised fundraising. Trustees wishing to take this course of action will need to obtain appropriate legal advice.

---

**PROPOSED CHANGES – FUNDRAISING REGULATIONS**

The Cabinet Office Strategy Unit has recommended that a new body should be established to develop voluntary sector self-regulation of fundraising under a voluntary code of practice. The Unit has also proposed that the Home Secretary should have the power to introduce statutory regulation if self-regulation does not prove effective. Legislation will be required to confer this power.

---

### Employing consultants and joint promotions

Employing external fundraisers and working with businesses are attractive options for charities that need to raise money on an ad hoc 'big

**NOTE**

The Charity Commission uses the term 'professional fundraisers' to describe external fundraising consultants. We have not used that term here in order to avoid confusion with professional fundraising staff employed by the charity as part of the staff team.

hit' approach, perhaps to fund a new development or give a cash boost to organisational running costs. Longer term relationships with corporate sponsors are also possible and can offer charities a degree of financial stability.

As with all fundraising approaches, trustees need ensure that the reward justifies the effort, so if fundraising consultants are to be employed, the trustees must be confident that this will represent good value for money.

When working with businesses on fundraising exercises (e.g. where a company makes a donation for every product sold), the trustees will need to consider additional wider issues, such as whether the charity wishes to be associated with the company or product sold, and the company's motivation. For example will the association be interpreted as the charity endorsing one manufacturer at the expense of another? Are the known business practices of the company (known as the 'commercial partici-pator') and the product sold compatible with the charity's objectives? Is the commercial participator seeking to use the relationship to promote sales or to target a specific market and, if so, is the charity comfortable with this?

**CASE EXAMPLE**

A children's welfare charity was approached by a sweet manufacturer who wanted to promote a new product by donating 1p of every sale to the charity. Although this did not directly contradict the charity's objectives, the trustees were concerned that the relationship would not be compatible with the work they had been undertaking with parents regarding healthy family eating within a limited budget. The trustees declined the opportunity.

Trustees should also consider the VAT implications of any sponsorship arrangements (see chapter 8).

Where trustees decide that engaging a fundraising consultant or entering an association with a commercial participator is worthwhile, they will need to comply with certain regulations, including:

1 defining the relationship by a written agreement in a prescribed format (see p. 203);
2 arrangements for the transfer of funds raised to the charity;
3 informing potential donors of the proportion of the donation that will be paid to the fundraiser; and
4 giving information to the public describing the benefit to the charity from the relationship with a commercial participator.

It is recommended that, as a matter of good practice, charities adopt these requirements in relation to any subsidiary trading companies.

## Selecting consultants

We have looked at the appointment of external professionals in earlier chapters of this book in relation to board appraisal (chapter 4) and investment fund managers (chapter 8) and many of the same principles apply to fundraising consultants. Trustees should first determine the role of the consultant, for example, whether the consultant will be developing or implementing strategy and whether the consultant will be responsible for a complete campaign or elements within the campaign (e.g. events, donor development or grant applications). The trustees will then need to identify a number of appropriate individuals, perhaps through names provided by an umbrella body such as NCVO (the National Council for Voluntary Organisations) or the Institute of Fundraising. Against each individual they should consider the following issues:

- relevant qualifications;
- experience, including experience of similar campaigns in comparable organisations;
- success record;
- sympathy with the charity and its culture;
- arrangements for monitoring activities and reporting to the trustees;
- cost.

Consultants' fees may be determined in a number of ways, including flat fees and commission based on a percentage of the total amount of money raised.

## Standard agreements

The requirements for agreements between charities and their fundraising consultants and commercial participators are laid down by statute. All such agreements must be made in writing and be signed by both parties.

The agreement, whether with a fundraising consultant or commercial participator, must contain the following information:

- the name and address of each party;
- the date and period of the agreement;
- terms regarding the variation or early termination of the agreement;
- the objectives of the agreement and the methods to be used in achieving those objectives;
- if more than one charity is involved in the agreement, the proportion of benefit to each charity (e.g. will the funds raised be equally divided or will there be a weighted split?); and
- provision for the amount of remuneration or expenses to be paid to the fundraiser or participator under the agreement and the method for calculating the amount (e.g. a percentage of funds raised or a flat amount).

In addition, for commercial participators, the agreement should cover the following:

- the proportion of the sale price that will be given to the charity or the donations that will be made; and
- a description of the type of contributions which will be made and of the circumstances in which they will be made.

Fundraisers and commercial participators' documents and other records relating to the agreement should be available to the charity. Funds raised under the agreement should be paid to the charity within 28 days of receipt.

The Institute of Fundraising has developed model agreements for relationships between charities and commercial participators and between charities and professional fundraisers.

# **10** Monitoring, evaluation and quality

## INTRODUCTION

The pressures of delivering and developing a charity's services often mean that trustees and senior staff have little time to reflect. The result can be that the charity becomes stuck on its particular treadmill and grows stale and out of date. Monitoring and evaluation of the charity's work and structures can be easily overlooked but are crucial to ensuring the charity's continued relevance and helping the trustees to plan for survival and growth. They are also key tools in the delivery of quality services. As such, monitoring and evaluation represent a key element of the trustee's role.

In this chapter, we will consider the value of monitoring and evaluation and look at some of the tools available, including 'off the shelf' models and quality standards. We will also look at some of the pitfalls to avoid when monitoring and evaluating the charity's services.

## DEFINITIONS

*Monitoring.* Monitoring is the ongoing measurement and interpretation of information. It is the process of collecting the data that will be used to measure current activities and their impact and to inform any review of the work.

*Evaluation.* Evaluation is a 'stop and look' periodic assessment of the organisation and/or its work. It involves considering outcomes against the wider context, objectives and targets and analysing the reasons behind successes and failures, identifying alternative approaches and future developments.

Monitoring and evaluation are considered together because they are co-dependent. Monitoring can stand on its own and is an extremely useful governance and management information tool if properly used. However, it is not possible to carry out a proper evaluation without having the necessary information on which to base your assessment.

## Why?

It used to be relatively easy for charities to tick along, day after day, year after year, believing that they were doing good work. If beneficiaries kept coming back to use the service and never, or only occasionally, complained, then charities often assumed that the beneficiaries were happy. This overlooks the fact that beneficiaries may recognise that a poor service is better than no service and disregards the reasons why they may not complain, for example for fear of losing the service or receiving prejudicial treatment as a result. This places the charity at risk of failing to meet its objects properly and of losing funds, beneficiaries, staff and volunteers to more effective providers.

A certain amount of ad hoc monitoring may give the organisation some useful feedback on the service, but will never truly be adequate for planning purposes. A structured programme of monitoring and evaluation is needed to ensure that the service is meeting objectives, identify any unmet need, and target areas for improvement. As well as measuring the success or otherwise of individual projects or services, monitoring and evaluation tools should be used to assess the performance of the organisation as a whole and to focus on individual elements of the charity's internal functioning. This may include consideration of the impact of a change to the governance structure or the introduction of revised policies.

Increased competition for funds, higher expectations from funders and greater public scrutiny of charities have forced many organisations to take monitoring, evaluation and quality measures seriously but trustees should not view this as a chore imposed by external pressures. The use of evaluation and quality standards as a means of demonstrating the organisation's validity to external stakeholders should be seen very much as a secondary benefit. Monitoring and evaluation are essential tools if an organisation is to develop and this is their primary purpose. Together with quality measures, monitoring and evaluation can raise the standards and performance of an organisation. If properly carried out, these can be a valuable tool which trustees can use to help to identify problems faced by the charity and to highlight and celebrate good practice and successes. The information gathered will also help trustees to manage staff effectively and to value their contributions, and to plan for the future.

## What to measure

Before any monitoring and evaluation process can begin, trustees need to identify what is to be measured and assessed. To do this they need to know the aims of both the 'thing' being measured, be that a structural change within the organisation, a new policy or a service, and the standards that they expect to be achieved. This will determine the focus of the monitoring or evaluation exercise. It may be helpful at this stage to look at outputs and outcomes and their bearing on efficiency and effectiveness.

Boards of trustees need to set their expectations in terms of organisational achievement in relation to outputs (i.e. the amount of work done), outcomes (i.e. the impact of that work) and organisational process, e.g. customer care. Some expectations may be purely quantitative, the 'how many', 'how long' type questions. This can be extremely useful information, helping identify, for example, areas of poor take up and levels of need. This form of monitoring is commonly used by charities,

---

**OUTPUTS AND OUTCOMES**

*Output* is the product of an activity, e.g. the number of presentations given or the number of clients seen. There is limited opportunity for quality measurement within output but it is useful in demonstrating efficiency, e.g. by considering the number of clients seen against the cost of the service or the resources available.

*Outcome* is the result of the activity. Ideally, this should relate to the original aims and reflect what you were hoping to achieve. For example, a welfare benefits advice service would hope to see an increase in benefit take up amongst its clients, and a drug rehabilitation project would hope to see a reduction in drug use. Monitoring outcomes is a means of measuring the effectiveness of the project. Outcomes are usually quality related and can be very difficult to monitor. This may be because a voluntary organisations is aiming for preventative or long-term benefits (at what point do you say a project to reduce youth offending is successful?) or because it can be hard to establish causality between the work of the organisation and the outcome. Outcome measurement can also be problematic because although the desired outcome may not be achieved, there may still be other positive results.

particularly to collect referral information such as gender, age, ethnicity, postcode and presenting problems.

However this type of output-driven, number crunching, approach is rarely adequate on its own. A qualitative element may be required in order for the monitoring to have any real meaning. The fact that a particular client has used your information service five times is not necessarily a good sign: it may mean that the client did not get what he or she wanted on the first four occasions. The trustees should set quality standards which describe the level which an activity, service or product must attain. Once the standards have been agreed, the charity will need to monitor performance against these standards and performance indicators may be used as a numerical measure of the degree to which the standard, outcome, or any other objective, is being achieved.

Quality standards and performance indicators may be used across the range of an organisation's work. It may be that trustees decide that every donation should be acknowledged within five working days or that clients receiving domiciliary care should not receive care services from more than three separate care workers in any six-week period. The standards should be monitored regularly so that trends can be identified, whether these are improvements in a service provided or declining performance. In this way, a set of performance indicators that cuts across the different areas of work can serve as a valuable tool for trustees in pre-empting and tracking problems and prioritising areas of concern.

In recognition of the fact that you will not get it right all of the time, you may also want to set targets for your performance indicators. These targets could be set to increase over time as improvements in service are anticipated. The case study on p. 208 illustrates how trustees can use the aims of the service to develop quality standards and performance indicators that then determine the information to be collected for monitoring and evaluation.

As can be seen from the case study, setting quality standards and performance indicators that are related to the aims automatically leads to certain information being collected. The same approach can be used for intended outcomes. The table on p. 208 illustrates how organisations can work through their aims and intended outcomes and/or quality standards in order to identify what they are measuring and the information they need to collect in order to monitor it.

**CASE EXAMPLE**

A charity running a respite care service for carers of people suffering with dementia has the reliability of the service as one of its aims. The trustees appreciate the stresses placed on the carers and recognise that missed appointments and lateness cause additional stress. Consequently they have developed a quality standard that says that appointments will not be cancelled with less than 24 hours' notice and that care assistants will arrive for appointments within 10 minutes of the agreed time. The service was temporarily short staffed and staff sickness and holidays made it difficult to provide a totally reliable service. In response, the trustees set a target that the reliability standard would be met in relation to 75 per cent of appointments for the first month, rising to 90 per cent for the following month when new staff would be in post. The achievement against these targets would represent the organisation's performance indicators, and 80 per cent reliability in the first month would indicate that the organisation had performed above its target.

In order to monitor performance against these standards and targets the charity kept details of all appointments attended (including the time of arrival) and all appointments cancelled, including the time of cancellation.

| Example | New equal opportunities policy | Customer service standards |
|---|---|---|
| Aim of service or policy | To promote the take up of services by minority ethnic groups | Provide a timely response to queries |
| Quality standard or intended outcome | Intended outcome of policy: number of people from minority ethnic groups using the service to be proportional to the local demographic | Quality standard: respond to telephone and email queries within four hours and to letters within two working days |
| Performance indicator | Increase take up from current level (5%) to 10% in year 1 and 17% in year 2 | Respond to 80% of telephone and email queries within four hours and 95% of letters within two working days |
| What information to collect | Ethnicity of service users | Date and time of incoming queries, method of query and date and time of response |

Do not forget that qualitative monitoring can include user satisfaction and the views of other stakeholders. This is discussed in the next section.

If you do not meet your performance indicator targets – ask why. There could be a valid reason, or it could indicate a flaw in your services or systems.

Do not reinvent the wheel – there are a number of widely available quality models that your charity could use or adapt. Some of these are discussed towards the end of this chapter.

## How?

Some charities see monitoring and evaluation as an inconvenience, but it need not be so. As has been demonstrated in this chapter, monitoring and evaluation is fundamental to the delivery of charitable objectives. If applied as an 'add on' to the charity's workload, any monitoring system can be awkward to administer; instead, monitoring arrangements should be integral to the work of the organisation and the planning of new services and projects. The examples used above showed how monitoring and evaluation are founded in the objectives of the work, so the actual process of monitoring should be based within the administration system. For example, referral procedures should collect all the information required for monitoring purposes and client reviews should include provision for recording the views of beneficiaries. Systems should be integrated into the charity's regular administration for the purposes of capturing statistical data whilst the 'soft' or qualitative monitoring can take place through other means, such as regular surveys and user groups. Integrating monitoring into regular activities in this way should add value to the charity's work, rather than get in the way of services.

Different services or activities will lend themselves to different approaches. It may not be possible to keep client records for confidential helplines but this would be appropriate for care or training projects. Group discussion may be the best approach for those who have difficulty with written language but surveys would be better suited for services that are spread over a wide geographical area.

Analysing all this data may seem daunting and should be done a bit at a time. Data collection should be designed in a way that makes information easy to retrieve. Similarly, monitoring information should be

## APPROACHES TO MONITORING

*Hard monitoring* (quantitative measures, statistics etc.)
- Diary records i.e. what happened each day
- Client records
- Records by staff member or volunteer who delivers service

*Soft monitoring* (qualitative measures, views and impact)
- Surveys and questionnaires
- Group discussion
- Individual discussion

*Sampling* – where it is not possible or practicable to collect monitoring information on every user, sample a cross section of the activity, e.g. every 10th user or every user for a week each month.

*Piloting* – rather than introduce a new monitoring system across the board and permanently, try piloting it. This could involve, for example, testing a new data collection form with one team of staff or for a limited period before reviewing and editing it to make it more user friendly and useful. Alternatively, ask a group of users to complete a pilot survey before rolling the form out across the user sample.

*Consistency* – for monitoring information to have any value it must be consistent, otherwise it will not be measuring like with like. This means client records should contain the same classes of information for each client and group discussions should cover the same ground each time. Forms and agendas can be designed to facilitate this. This does not prevent additional information being recorded, and space should be made in any monitoring system for a wider range of information to be recorded as necessary, e.g. a space for notes on a client's records or for additional comments on a questionnaire.

*Review* – monitoring arrangements should be reviewed on a periodic basis. Are the arrangements providing you with the information you need?

presented to trustees in a way that is readily understandable. Tables and graphs can often illustrate findings more effectively than text, e.g. cross tables can be used to show a number of factors together, such as a breakdown of clients by location and presenting problem.

Methods of evaluation will be based on the foundation of data collection and canvassing views. Evaluations should, however, be more thorough than monitoring, covering a wider range of issues and stakeholders. They may, for example, look at whether the service is innovative, whether it should be more outcome focussed and should take in the opinions of staff, volunteers, trustees, users and partner agencies. An evaluation will also pay greater attention to the wider context, e.g. professional standards, academic opinion and accepted best practice. Findings and opinions may be presented to stakeholders for discussion at various points throughout the evaluation in order to refine understanding, culminating in a written report.

Given that monitoring and evaluation should be included in a project from the outset, arrangements and budgeting will be integral to project planning and should be considered within funding applications.

## Internal or external evaluation?

Although many organisations conduct their own monitoring and evaluation processes, external evaluation may offer a fresh approach and objectivity. This can be particularly useful for demonstrating the value of a service within the wider external context. Charities may implement a degree of external evaluation themselves by measuring outputs against regional or national figures, but an evaluation conducted by an independent and external organisation or individual offers a completely objective account of the charity's work.

Similar arrangements exist in relation to quality standards. We have already discussed the need for charities to develop their own quality standards, but 'off the shelf' standards can provide an objective check and opportunities for comparison with other organisations. Some of the widely available quality measures are discussed later in this chapter.

We have considered the use of external consultants before, and the discussion in chapter 5 in relation to externally conducted board appraisal will be equally relevant here. Evaluation can be a sensitive issue and it is easy for those involved in the charity to complain about the evaluator if they do not like what has been said. In selecting an external evaluator, it is important to be particularly alert to the individual's experience with your type of organisation and his or her empathy with the concerns of all involved. Consider how the evaluator will involve staff and volunteers in the process and, crucially, how the trustees will retain ownership of the evaluation. Ownership is not just about the final publication of the evaluation report, it is also concerned with ensuring that evaluation remains relevant, is accepted by the charity, and that it is controlled by the trustees, in partnership with the external evaluator.

---

**tip**

Any externally conducted evaluation should be subject to written terms of reference, describing the purpose, process and timescale of the evaluation as well as other crucial issues such as ownership, interim reporting and publication.

---

## Process

As has been discussed above, monitoring should be an ongoing process of collecting data which is to be presented to the board or senior staff in order to allow them to measure progress and make adjustments as necessary. In this sense, monitoring forms part of management and governance information in much the same way as do management accounts (see chapter 7).

In terms of quality standards, internal standards are often developed and implemented by a subcommittee of trustees, supported by senior and operational staff. External standards, as discussed later in this chapter, may well define the process to be followed.

Evaluations can be complex and lengthy and it is useful to set a timescale for any evaluation exercise before it starts. Working backwards (i.e. from the date on which it is expected that the evaluation will be completed) gives a strong indication of the workload and viability of the exercise. The process will involve reading background information, collecting and analysing all relevant statistical data and canvassing the views of a variety of stakeholders. Once the analysis and opinion forming is underway, it will be necessary to test preliminary findings with the relevant parties to ensure the accuracy of views and gather any wider contextual information. There may be valid justifications for practices that initially appear to be questionable. Draft reports will need to be presented to trustees and others and amended as necessary. Throughout the process, trustees should be kept informed and involved. The process normally concludes with a final written report, which may be supported by presentations to relevant internal and external stakeholders. It is critical to any monitoring and evaluation exercise that findings are communicated to the organisation as a whole.

## Potential problems

### 'You get what you measure'

In developing monitoring and evaluation procedures trustees should be aware that there is a risk that 'you get what you measure', i.e. staff will focus on the areas that they know are being monitored, for example increased recruitment of black and minority ethnic volunteers, at the expense of areas of work that are not under review. Alternatively, whilst the targets may be achieved, the anticipated improvements may not result, e.g. the charity may be successful in recruiting more volunteers from black and minority ethnic groups, but may not retain them. Consequently trustees will need to develop a more sophisticated approach, such as specifying not only targets for recruitment of volunteers, but also retention.

Monitoring the outcomes of services enables trustees to identify the impact of the charity's work, but the 'you get what you measure'

---

**CASE EXAMPLE**

An charity ran a supported employment scheme for the long-term unemployed. The scheme involved securing temporary work placements for clients, with the aim of improving self-esteem and confidence, developing new skills and adapting back into employment. In accordance with its objects, the charity focussed on unemployed people from high need groups, including people with disabilities and those with a history of homelessness, substance misuse or mental ill health. It originally evaluated its success based on the number of people matched in temporary placements and achieving positive outcomes following the completion of the placement. Given the nature of the client group, these outcomes could be quite modest, for example clients moving onto voluntary work or maintaining the social support networks developed during the placement. A change in the requirements imposed by the funder, which redefined a positive outcome as gaining permanent employment, completely changed the nature of the scheme. The charity was influenced by the evaluation requirements to move away from providing for the high need group of long-term unemployed people to those more likely to find work at the conclusion of the placement.

approach can be particularly dangerous here, as the pressure to perform to targets may unduly influence the direction of the service.

The case study on p. 213 not only illustrates the risk that 'you get what you measure' but also the concern that funders may drive monitoring and evaluation requirements and consequently influence the nature of the service. It is entirely appropriate that funders should require organisations to monitor and evaluate the work that they fund. They need to know that their money is being spent on the purposes for which it was given and is achieving the desired end results. However, trustees must ensure that these monitoring requirements do not pollute the charity's activities or divert it from its objects. In the example above, the change in emphasis was introduced by the funder of the scheme and resulted in the charity working with a group of users that fell outside its beneficiary area. In accepting the funding on these terms and consequently being unduly influenced by these requirements, the trustees may well have acted in breach of trust.

## Resistance

Many people within charities, from the board to the volunteers, see monitoring, evaluation and quality measures as challenging and even threatening. They may consider that their own work is being inspected or questioned or that the service or project is being evaluated in order to identify potential funding cuts. Equally, they may simply resent any extra work involved. For these reasons any programme should be introduced sensitively and the objectives and subsequent findings clearly communicated to all participants. An exercise that is committed to celebrating successes, acknowledging difficulties, and giving opportunities for learning and improving, is likely to find a warmer reception than a 'justify yourself' approach.

## Bad news

Trustees, given their leadership role, should consider how they would respond to any negative findings of a monitoring, evaluation or quality programme. Whilst the whole point of the work is to pinpoint problems and identify remedial action, what would happen if the results were worse than expected? How would operational staff and volunteers be supported in addressing such findings? Trustees should receive interim progress reports on any evaluation exercise in order to prepare for any difficult issues that might arise.

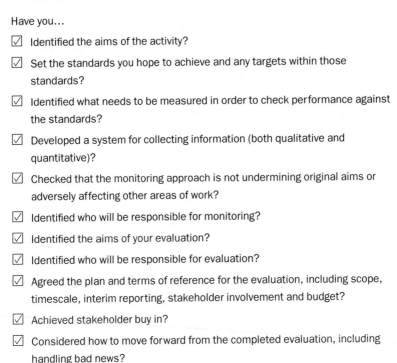

## CHECKLIST

Have you...

- ☑ Identified the aims of the activity?
- ☑ Set the standards you hope to achieve and any targets within those standards?
- ☑ Identified what needs to be measured in order to check performance against the standards?
- ☑ Developed a system for collecting information (both qualitative and quantitative)?
- ☑ Checked that the monitoring approach is not undermining original aims or adversely affecting other areas of work?
- ☑ Identified who will be responsible for monitoring?
- ☑ Identified the aims of your evaluation?
- ☑ Identified who will be responsible for evaluation?
- ☑ Agreed the plan and terms of reference for the evaluation, including scope, timescale, interim reporting, stakeholder involvement and budget?
- ☑ Achieved stakeholder buy in?
- ☑ Considered how to move forward from the completed evaluation, including handling bad news?

## Quality

The voluntary sector often tries to distinguish itself from other service providers on the basis of quality. As has been discussed earlier in this chapter, there is a risk of charities becoming stale. An active commitment to quality ensures that organisations are constantly striving to improve, both internally and in relation to the services provided. The Quality Standards Task Group (QSTG) run by the National Council for Voluntary Organisations (NCVO) describes a quality voluntary group as one that seeks continuous improvement, works to meet requirements that have been agreed with third parties, promotes equal opportunities, is accountable, and adds value.

## Quality models

There are a number of different ready-made models for quality management and validation. Each model is based on a documented system designed to measure practices against standards and to promote improvement. Organisations may choose to adopt one of these rather than develop their own systems. As the models consider different elements of organisational function, it is important to identify the model which is most appropriate for the charity in question.

The advantage of these models is that they demonstrate a charity's commitment to quality and ongoing organisational improvement. In the case of those that are externally evaluated, the models also show that the charity has attained a nationally (or in some cases internationally) recognised standard. Although the process of attaining and maintaining the standards can be hard work and time consuming, it should also serve to improve the governance and management of the organisation, the quality of the service and the morale and involvement of staff and volunteers. Trustees should, therefore, view these models as a means of achieving continuous improvement, rather than a badge to be worn for the benefit of funders or other stakeholders.

## PQASSO

The Practical Quality Assurance System for Small Organisations (PQASSO) was designed by Charities Evaluation Services specifically for small to medium-sized voluntary organisations. It can also be used to measure the quality of projects or branches within larger charities. The system promotes continuous improvement and is comprehensive, covering all aspects of organisations' work with the focus on the following areas:

- governance and management;
- staff and volunteers;
- planning for quality;
- managing money and resources;
- managing activities;
- user-centred service;
- training and development;
- networking and partnership;

- monitoring and evaluation; and
- results.

PQASSO takes the form of a self-assessment workpack, giving flexibility and allowing organisations to implement quality management at their own pace. PQASSO has been costed to reflect the market and as such it is an affordable model for small groups.

## Business Excellence Model

Like PQASSO, the Business Excellence Model considers all elements of organisational activity. Unlike PQASSO (and as the name implies) the Business Excellence Model was originally designed for the corporate sector, however it has been implemented by public sector organisations and voluntary groups. This is a Europe-wide tool and is also known as the EFQM Excellence Model. EFQM is the European Foundation for Quality Management. The model is administered in the UK by the British Quality Foundation, itself a not-for-profit organisation.

The Business Excellence Model is based on continuous improvement through a regular self-assessment which looks at what the organisation (or a project or division within an organisation) does and what it achieves. Areas considered include leadership, policy, strategy, partnerships, people, resources and results, including the social impact.

The cost of implementing the model varies greatly, depending on the degree of implementation. Although a basic self-assessment can be done fairly cheaply, more rigorous appraisals can become very expensive, particularly if external consultants are asked to support the assessment process.

Registered charities can join the British Quality Foundation for a reduced fee. Membership gives access to networking groups and a range of information.

## Charter Mark

The Charter Mark Award is a government run quality model that focuses on customer service. Designed for statutory services it is also available to voluntary organisations that provide services to the public and receive at least 10 per cent of their income through public sector funding.

The Charter Mark scheme is being revised in 2003, with the original ten criteria being reduced to six and changes to the assessment process.

The revised scheme is due to be launched late in 2003 and trustees wishing to use this quality model are advised to check the Charter Mark website for the most up to date information (see www.chartermark.gov.uk).

The new criteria include consideration of the organisation's contribution to enhancing opportunity and quality of life in their communities and the assessment process includes a web-based self-assessment package which will be flexible and accessible for Charter Mark applicants.

## ISO 9000

ISO 9000 is the collective name for a group of international standards for quality management systems. Issues considered under the standard include the organisation's quality management system, management responsibility, the management of resources, the end product or service, and monitoring and improvement. The standard considers not only whether appropriate quality management systems are in place, but also whether the standards are being consistently applied.

Those wishing to register for the standard have to prepare a quality manual and supporting procedures to ensure implementation. The award is subject to external assessment by a registering body. Once registered, the quality management systems of organisations holding the standard are reviewed periodically.

ISO 9000 is not cheap, being subject to initial assessment fees and an annual fee, and is only appropriate for larger voluntary groups.

### Investors in People

Investors in People (IIP) is a national cross-sector standard concerned with the training and development of people within an organisation or project. The standard is focussed on training and development as a means of achieving organisational objectives and is based on the four principles of:

1  commitment to invest in people;
2  planning the development of people;
3  taking action on development in relation to objectives; and
4  evaluating the outcomes of training and development.

Organisations must provide evidence of how they meet the four principles and the standard is awarded subject to external assessment. An initial assessment that identifies areas where the required standard has not been met is usually carried out, with a further assessment before the standard is awarded. Once an organisation has IIP status, it is subject to periodic review.

There is a charge for assessments so the total cost will vary depending on the size of the organisation, length of assessment etc. Given the nature of this model, charities are unlikely to seek IIP unless they have a significant staff or volunteer team.

**Which model?**

| Model | What it measures | Who is it suitable for? |
| --- | --- | --- |
| PQASSO | Across organisation | Small to medium voluntary groups |
| Business Excellence Model | Across organisation | Larger organisations, although a more low key implementation may be appropriate for smaller groups |
| Chartermark | Customer services | All |
| ISO 9000 | Quality management | Large groups |
| Investors in People | Training and development of people within the organisation | Medium to large groups with significant staff/volunteer teams |
| Service-specific models | Quality of service delivery | All, although much will depend on the model in question |

**Service-specific models**

Trustees should also consider whether there are any quality assurance or management systems that are specific to the type of service that they offer. For example, advice services may apply for the Community Legal Service's Quality Mark. In some circumstances, achieving a service-specific quality standard may be a condition of funding.

# Benchmarking

We have looked at monitoring and evaluation as an internal exercise, with organisations considering performance against self-created standards and by measurement against an external, common standard. We have also considered external, independent evaluation. A further option is for organisations to compare themselves against other groups or businesses through benchmarking.

Benchmarking involves comparing different aspects of the work of a group of organisations. It can be a very flexible approach. You can compare services, products or processes; you can look at a wide range of issues or focus on areas of concern; and you can benchmark with similar organisations or take a cross-sector approach on common issues such as customer care. Benchmarking may take place as a one-off exercise or be an ongoing relationship.

The benchmarking process should be a mutually beneficial relationship, with every organisation in the benchmarking group being able to learn and develop from the experience of others.

**tip**

If undertaking a benchmarking exercise, be sure that all parties are in agreement as to the scope of the review and what will be done with the information – will it be confidential to those in the benchmarking group?

**PROPOSED CHANGES – BENCHMARKING**

The Cabinet Office Strategy Unit has recommended, as part of its review of charity law, that groups of voluntary organisations that deliver similar services should consider developing common performance indicators and benchmarking for their area of work.

# Directory

## General reference

Adirondack, Sandy & Sinclair Taylor, James (consulting eds) *The Voluntary Sector Legal Handbook* (Sinclair Taylor & Martin Solicitors, Directory of Social Change, 2001) (2nd ed)

Adirondack, Sandy *Just About Managing? Effective management for voluntary organisations and community groups* (London Voluntary Service Council, 1998) (3rd ed)

Claricoat, John & Philips, Hilary *Charity Law A–Z, Key Questions Answered* (Jordans, 1998)

ICSA Best Practice Guide *Guide to Guarantee Companies*

Leatherdale, Malcolm *How to Run Your Charity: The Role of the Charity Secretary* (ICSA Publishing Ltd, 1998)

NCVO *The Company Right or Wrong? The pros and cons of incorporation for charities and other voluntary organisations* (NCVO, 1997)

Reason, Jacki (ed) *The Charities Manual* (ICSA Publishing Ltd, looseleaf)

For up-to-date information on the proposed changes in charity law and the new forms of incorporation for not-for-profit organisations check the voluntary sector press, particularly:

Wednesday's *Guardian:* www.SocietyGuardian.co.uk

*Third Sector:* www.thirdsector.co.uk

*Charity Finance:* www.charityfinance.co.uk

### Charity Commission
The Charity Commission makes its guidance booklets available on its website www.charitycommission.gov.uk. The most relevant are:

| | |
|---|---|
| CC2 | *Charities and the Charity Commission* |
| CC3 | *Responsibilities of Charity Trustees* |
| CC4 | *Charities for the Relief of the Poor* |
| CC6 | *Charities for the Relief of Sickness* |

CC9     *Political Activities and Campaigning by Charities*
CC9a    *Political Activities and Campaigning by Local Community Charities*
CC11   *Payment of Charity Trustees*
CC21   *Registering as a Charity*
CC23   *Exempt Charities*
CC25   *Resolving Charity Disputes: Our role*
CC45   *Central Register of Charities*
CC47   *Inquiries into Charities*
CC47(a)  *Inquiries into Charities: Your rights and obligations*

The Commission has been conducting a review of the register of charities, considering issues such as the different charitable purposes. A range of review documents are available, including:
RR7   *The Independence of Charities from the State*
RR8   *The Public Character of Charity*

**Companies House**
GBF1   *Company Formation*
GBF2   *Company Names*

## Trustee responsibilities

### Health and safety

ACEVO *Health and Safety: Basic guide to good practice*
Eastwood, Mike *The Charity Trustee's Handbook* (Directory of Social Change, 2001)
Hinde, Al & Kavanagh, Charlie (Jill Barlow, ed) *The Health & Safety Handbook for Voluntary & Community Organisations* (Directory of Social Change, 2001)

**Charity Commission**
CC3   *Responsibility of Charity Trustees*

**Companies House**
GBA1   *Directors and Secretaries Guide*

**Health and Safety Executive**
*An introduction to health and safety*
*RIDDOR Explained: Reporting of Injuries, Diseases and Dangerous Occurrences Regulations*
*Work-related stress: a short guide*
*Health and safety regulation: A short guide*
*First aid at work: Your questions answered*

## Marketing

Ali, Moi *The New DIY Guide to Marketing* (ICSA Publishing Ltd, 2001)
Bruce, Ian *Successful Charity Marketing* (ICSA Publishing Ltd, 1998)

## Risk management

ACEVO *Risk Management: Basic guide to good practice*
Clark, Caroline *Managing Risk – Guidelines for Medium-sized Voluntary Organisations* (NCVO, 2001)
ICSA Best Practice Guide *Managing Conflicts of Interest in the Not-for-profit Sector*

## Planning

ACEVO: *Strategic planning: Basic guide to good practice*
Lawrie, Alan *The complete guide to business and strategic planning for voluntary organisations* (Directory of Social Change, 2001) (2nd ed)

## Data protection

Ticher, Paul *Data Protection for Voluntary Organisations* (Directory of Social Change, 2002)
Clark, Osborne *A practical guide to data protection* (ICSA Publishing Ltd, 2002)

## Campaigning

Latimer, Mark *The Campaigning Handbook* (Directory of Social Change)
Gray, John F & Elsden, Stephen *Organising Special Events for Fundraising and Campaigning* (Directory of Social Change and Charities Aid Foundation, 2000)

Reason, Jacki, Hayes, Ruth & Forbes, Duncan *Voluntary but not Amateur* (London Voluntary Service Council, 2000)
Lamb, Brian *Good Campaigns Guide* (NCVO, 1997)

## Recruitment, appointment and induction of trustees

Akpeki, Tesse *Getting on board: Strategies for finding and supporting trustees* (NCVO, 1997)
Akpeki, Tesse *Recruiting and supporting black and minority ethnic trustees* (NCVO, 2001)
NCVO *Trustee bank: A directory of trustee brokerage services* (free booklet)
Nunan, Kevin *The Good Trustee Guide* (NCVO, 1999) (3rd ed)

**ICSA Best Practice Guides**
*The Appointment and Induction of Charity Trustees*
*ICSA Model Code of Conduct for Charity Trustees*
*ICSA Model Job Description for Charity Trustees*

**Charity Commission**
*Welcome to New Trustees*
CC11    *Payment of Charity Trustees*
CC24    *Users on Board: Beneficiaries who become trustees*
RS1    *Trustee recruitment, selection and induction*

## Board of trustees

Adirondack, Sandy *The Good Governance Action Plan for Voluntary Organisations* (NCVO, 1999)
Adirondack, Sandy *The Good Governance Action Plan for Medium and Large Voluntary Organisations* (NCVO, 2000)
Balkam, Steve *Assessing Your Board's Performance: a DIY guide to board self-evaluation* (NCVO, 1994)
Belbin, Meredith *Management Teams – Why they succeed or fail* (Butterworth Heinemann, 1981)
Belbin, Meredith *Team Roles at Work* (Butterworth Heinemann)
Comer, Lee & Ticher, Paul *The Minute Taker's Handbook* (Directory of Social Change, 2002)

Hudson, Mike *Managing Without Profit: the art of managing third sector organisations* (Penguin Books, 1999) (2nd ed) (available from the Directory of Social Change)

Morgan, Gareth G. *The Charity Treasurer's Handbook* (Directory of Social Change, 2002)

**ICSA Guidance Notes**
*ICSA Model Job Description for Chair of the Board of Trustees*
*ICSA Model Job Description for a Treasurer*
*ICSA Model Job Description for the Secretary of the Board*

**ACEVO publications**
*Partners in Leadership : A new style of governance and management for charities*
*Duties of a Company Secretary: Basic guide to good practice*

## Meetings and governing documents

**Charity Commission**

| | |
|---|---|
| CC22 | *Choosing and Preparing a Governing Document* |
| CC36 | *Amending Charities' Governing Documents: Orders and Schemes* |
| CC48 | *Charities and meetings* |
| GD1, GD2, GD3 | *Model governing documents* |

**Companies House**
GBA7   *Resolutions*

## People management

Akpeki, Tesse *Setting Chief Executive Remuneration* (NCVO, 2001)

Burnell, John *Managing People in Charities* (ICSA Publishing Ltd, 2001) (2nd ed)

Cook, Tim & Braithwaite, Guy *A Management Companion for Voluntary Organisations* (Directory of Social Change, 2000)

Harris, John *The Good Management Guide for the Voluntary Sector* (NCVO, 2002)

ICSA Best Practice Guide *Establishing a whistleblowing procedure*

NCVO *Current Practice, Good Practice: Guidelines for good practice on pay and remuneration for senior posts in the voluntary sector* (NCVO, 1996)

NCVO *Flexible Working Solutions* (NCVO, 2000)

NCVO *The Good Employment Guide for the Voluntary Sector* (NCVO, 2002) (3rd ed)

Taylor, Gill *Managing Recruitment & Selection* (Directory of Social Change, 1996)

Taylor, Gill & Thornton, Christine *Managing People* (Directory of Social Change, 1995)

### ACEVO publications

*Recruitment of chief executives to voluntary organisations: Basic guide to good practice*

*Contract of employment (including a model contract): Basic guide to good practice*

*Reward strategy: Basic guide to good practice*

*Staff handbooks: Basic guide to good practice*

*Working time regulations 1998: Basic guide to good practice*

*Disciplinary issues: Basic guide to good practice*

*Model documents pack*

*Partners in leadership: A new style of governance and management for charities*

*Leading the organisation: The relationship between chairs and chief executives*

### Charity Commission

CC60    *The Hallmarks of a Well-Run Charity*

## Financial management and control

ACEVO *Setting up a trading company: Basic guide to good practice*

Morgan, Gareth G. *The Charity Treasurer's Handbook* (Directory of Social Change, 2002)

NCVO *VAT for voluntary organisations: a step by step guide* (NCVO, 2001) (4th ed)

Poffley, Adrian *Financial Stewardship of Charities* (Directory of Social Change, 2002)

Randall, Adrian *The ICSA Guide to Charity Accounting: Revised SORP 2000 edition* (ICSA Publishing Ltd, 2001)

Sayer, Kate *Practical Guide to Charity Accounting* (Sayer Vincent and Directory of Social Change, 2003)

Sayer, Kate *Practical Guide to Financial Management for Charities* (Sayer Vincent and Directory of Social Change, 2002) (2nd ed)

Sayer, Kate *Practical Guide to VAT for Charities and Voluntary Organisations* (Sayer Vincent and Directory of Social Change, 2001) (2nd ed)

Wise, David *Accounting and Finance for Charities: For love and money* (ICSA Publishing Ltd, 1998)

*Charity Finance* (monthly journal) is useful reading. See also the website www.charityfinance.co.uk

**Charity Commission**

*Accounting and Reporting by Charities: Statement of Recommended Practice (Revised 2000)*

*Annual Return*

*Charities and Risk Management*

CC12   *Managing Financial Difficulties and Insolvency in Charities*

CC13   *The Official Custodian for Charities' Land Holding Service*

CC14   *Investment of Charitable Funds: Basic Principles*

CC19   *Charities' Reserves*

CC28   *Disposing of Charity Land*

CC33   *Acquiring Land*

CC35   *Charities and Trading*

CC42   *Appointing Nominees and Custodians: Guidance under s.19(4) of the Trustee Act 2000*

CC51   *Charity Accounts: The New Framework*

CC52   *Charity Accounts: Charities under £10,000 Threshold*

CC54   *Accounting for the Smaller Charity*

CC55   *Accruals Accounting for the Smaller Charity*

CC56   *The Carrying Out of an Independent Examination: Directions and Guidance Notes*

CC61   *Charity Accounts 2001: The framework*

CC63   *Independent Examination of Charities*

CC64   *Receipts and Payments Accounts Pack 2001*

CC65    *Accruals Accounts Pack August 2001*
CC66    *SORP 2000: Example reports and accounts*
CC8    *Internal Financial Controls for Charities*

**Companies House**
GBA2    *Annual Return*
GBA3    *Accounts and Accounting Reference Dates*
GBA4    *Auditors*
GBA5    *Late Filing Penalties*

**HM Customs & Excise**
*Notice 700/1    Should I be registered for VAT?*
*Notice 701/1    Charities*
*Notice 701/5    Clubs and associations*
*Notice 742    Land and property*

**Inland Revenue and HM Customs & Excise**
*CWL4    Fundraising Events: Exemptions for charities and other quali-
fying bodies*

**Inland Revenue**
*IR2001 Trading by Charities*
*Gift Aid Toolkit*

## Fundraising

Botting, Nina & Norton, Michael *The Complete Fundraising Handbook*
(Institute of Fundraising and Directory of Social Change, 2001)
Brown, Harry *Community Fundraising: The Effective Use of Volunteer
Networks* (Directory of Social Change, Charities Aid Foundation and
Institute of Fundraising, 2002)
Canning, Veronica *A practical guide to fundraising and public relations*
(ICSA Publishing Ltd, 1999)
Clay, Anthony (ed) *Trust Fundraising* (Directory of Social Change,
Charities Aid Foundation and Institute of Fundraising, 1999)
*The Fundraiser's Guide to the Law* (Bates, Wells & Braithwaite and
Centre for Voluntary Sector Development, Charities Aid Foundation
and Directory of Social Change, 2000)

Gilchrist, Karen & Horsley, Margo *Fundraising from Grant-making Trusts and Foundations* (Directory of Social Change and Charities Aid Foundation, 2000)

Gilchrist, Karen *Promoting Your Cause: A Guide for Fundraisers and Campaigners* (Directory of Social Change and Charities Aid Foundation)

Gray, John F & Elsden, Stephen *Organising Special Events for Fundraising and Campaigning* (Directory of Social Change and Charities Aid Foundation, 2000)

Home Office *Charitable Fund-raising: Professional and Commercial Involvement* (HMSO)

Institute of Fundraising *The Charity Donors' Charter*

Institute of Fundraising *Forms of Agreement and Model Contracts*

Morton, Valerie (ed) *Corporate Fundraising* (Directory of Social Change, Charities Aid Foundation and Institute of Fundraising, 2002) (2nd ed)

Mullin, Redmond *Fundraising Strategy* (Directory of Social Change, Charities Aid Foundation and Institute of Fundraising)

Passingham, Sarah *Organising Local Events* (Directory of Social Change and Institute of Fundraising, 1995) (2nd ed)

Passingham, Sarah *Tried and Tested Ideas for Raising Money Locally, Small and Medium-Scale Events* (Directory of Social Change, 1997) (2nd ed)

Sutherland, Jane & Eastwood, Mike *Raising Money for Good Causes* (North Kent CVS and Directory of Social Change, 1998)

Wilberforce, Sebastian (ed) *Legacy Fundraising: The Art of Seeking Bequests* (Directory of Social Change, Charities Aid Foundation and Institute of Fundraising, 2001) (2nd ed)

**Charity Commission**

CC20    *Charities and Fund-raising*

*Charities and Commercial Sponsorship* (see the 'Useful Guidelines' section of the Charity Commission website)

**Institute of Fundraising**

The Institute of Fundraising produces a wide range of Codes of Practice including:

*Acceptance and Refusal of Donations*

*Charities Working with Business*

*Charity Challenge Events*
*Code of Conduct*
*Fundraising on the Internet*
*Handling Cash Donations*
*House to House Collections*
*Legacy Fundraising*
*Management of Static Collection Boxes*
*Outdoor Fundraising Events in the UK*
*Payment of Fundraisers on a Commission Basis*
*Payroll Giving*
*Personal Solicitation for Committed Gifts*
*Raffles and Lotteries*
*Reciprocal Charity Mailings*
*Telephone Fundraising*

## Monitoring, evaluation and quality

British Quality Foundation *Assessing for Excellence: a practical guide for self-assessment* (British Quality Foundation, 1999)
Farley, Tony *Quality First: Quality Assurance Management for Community Organisations* (Birmingham Voluntary Service Council, 1999) (available from the Directory for Social Change)
VSNTO *A Guide to Investors in People for Voluntary Organisations in England & Wales* (Voluntary Sector National Training Organisation and Investors in People UK, 1999)
VSNTO *How To Become an Investor in People: A Guide for the Voluntary Sector* (Voluntary Sector National Training Organisation, 2002)
*How to improve your services: A Guide to Quality Schemes for the Public Sector* (Cabinet Office, 1999) (available at http://www.cabinet-office.gov.uk/servicefirst/)

### Charities Evaluation Services

Ellis, Jean *Practical monitoring and evaluation: a guide for voluntary organisations* (Charities Evaluation Services, 2002)
*First Steps in Quality* (Charities Evaluation Services, 2002)
*First Steps in Monitoring and Evaluation* (Charities Evaluation Services, 2002)
Connor, Anne *Monitoring Ourselves* (Charities Evaluation Services, 1999)

Van Der Eyken, Willem *Managing Evaluation* (Charities Evaluation
    Services, 1999)
A range of discussion papers is also available.

**Charity Commission**
*CC60 The Hallmarks of a Well-Run Charity*

**Quality Standards Task Group publications**
*Approaching Quality: A Guide to the Choices You Could Make* (NCVO,
    1999)
*Developing a quality policy* (NCVO)
*Excellence in View: A Guide to the European Foundation for Quality
    Management (EFQM) Excellence Model for the Voluntary Sector*
    (NCVO, 2000)
*Self-Assessment Workbook – Measuring Success* (NCVO, 2000)

## Web resources

**Accounting Standards Board**
    <www.asb.org.uk>

**Association of Chief Executives of Voluntary Organisations (ACEVO)**
    The professional association for chief executives in the third sector in
    England and Wales.
    <www.acevo.org.uk>

**Belbin**
    Details of Belbin's products and services.
    <www.belbin.info/>

**Benchmarking Centre**
    <www.benchmarking.co.uk>

**British Chambers of Commerce**
    <www.britishchambers.org.uk>

**British Quality Foundation**
    For information on the Business/EFQM Excellence Model. See also
    the European Foundation for Quality Management below.
    <www.quality-foundation.co.uk>

**British Standards Institution**
Information on ISO 9000.
<www.bsi.org.uk>

**Broadcasting Support Services**
For the Broadcast Appeals Consortium code of practice.
<www.bss.org>

**Business Link**
Information on Business Link, the national business advice service. The website includes information and factsheet on benchmarking and different quality models.
<www.businessadviceonline.org>

**Business in the Community (BITC)**
Encourages corporate social responsibility and business involvement in local communities, including employee volunteering.
<www.bitc.org.uk>

**Charities Evaluation Services**
Provides monitoring, evaluation and quality services to the voluntary sector, including consultancy, training, literature and PQASSO.
<www.ces-vol.org.uk>

**Charity Commission**
The statutory organisation that regulates charities in England and Wales. Provides guidance and advices to charities through its extensive range of publications, available free via its website.
<www.charitycommission.gov.uk>

**Charity Finance Directors' Group**
Helps charities to manage their accounting, taxation, audit and other finance related functions and promotes good practice
<www.cfdg.org.uk>

**Charter Mark**
<www.chartermark.gov.uk>

**Companies House**
The statutory body responsible for regulating the incorporation, re-registration and striking-off of companies and the registration of documents to be filed under company legislation.

**Compact Law**
Provides easily accessible information on employment law.
<www.compactlaw.co.uk/emp.html>

**Customs and Excise**
Useful publications and details of local VAT advice centres.
<www.hmce.gov.uk>

**Department of Trade and Industry**
Information on changes to company law and requirements in relation
to company secretaries. See also the DTI's *From Quality to Excellence*
website which provides a range of information on quality improvements.
<www.dti.gov.uk/>

**Directory of Social Change**
Provides information and training.
<www.dsc.org.uk>

**Ethnic Minority Foundation (EMF) and the Council of Ethnic Minority
Voluntary Organisations (CEMVO)**
Maintain a trustee register.
<www.emf-cemvo.co.uk>

**European Foundation for Quality Management**
<www.efqm.org>

**Federation of Small Businesses**
Provides advice on tax and VAT issues.
<www.fsb.org.uk>

**Financial Services Authority**
Information on different investment products and regulation.
<www.fsa.gov.uk>

**Gaming Board for Great Britain**
Requirements for regulating lotteries, bingo or other gaming events.
<www.gbgb.org.uk>

**HM Government**
Strategy Unit's *Private Action, Public Benefit* report can be found at:
<www.cabinet-office.gov.uk/innovation/2002/charity/report/
index.htm>

**Health and Safety Executive**
A wide range of useful leaflets are available free from the HSE.
<www.hse.gov.uk>

**Information Commissioner**
Information on the data protection principles.
<www.dataprotection.gov.uk>

**Inland Revenue**
A number of areas of this site are relevant including the employers'
section on National Insurance contributions.
<www.inlandrevenue.gov.uk>

**Industrial Common Ownership Movement (ICOM)**
The umbrella body for co-operatives.
E-mail: icom@icom.org.uk

**Institute of Chartered Secretaries and Administrators (ICSA)**
In addition to a number of useful publications and guidance notes, the
ICSA offers a trustee brokerage service through its trustee register.
<www.icsa.org.uk>

**Institute of Fundraising**
<www.institute-of-fundraising.org.uk>

**Institute of Quality Assurance**
<www.iqa.org>

**Investors in People**
<www.iipuk.co.uk/>

**Legal Services Commission**
Information on the Community Legal Service Quality Mark.
<www.legalservices.gov.uk/qmark/>

**National Council for Voluntary Organisations (NCVO)**
The umbrella body for the voluntary sector in England. Produces a
wide range of publications including good practice guides, training
manuals, research reports.
<www.ncvo-volorg.uk>

**Northern Ireland Council for Voluntary Action (NICVA)**
<www.nicva.org.uk>

## Occupational Pensions Regulatory Authority (OPRA)
Details of stakeholder pension providers.

## Quality Standards Task Group
Promotes quality and quality management in the voluntary sector.
<www.ncvo-vol.org.uk/asp/search/ncvo/main.aspx?siteID=1&sID=
7&documentID=258>

## Recruitment agencies include:
CF Appointments: www.charity-executives.co.uk
Charity Connections: www.charityconnections.co.uk
Charity Futures: www.charityfutures.com
Charity People: www.charitypeople.co.uk
Charity Recruitment: www.charityrecruitment.co.uk/home.html
Harris Hill: www.harrishill.co.uk

## Scottish Council for Voluntary Organisations (SCVO)
www.scvo.org.uk

## Small Business Service
<www.businessadviceonline.org>

## United Kingdom Accreditation Service
Details of accredited ISO 9000 certification bodies.
<www.ukas.com>

## Volresource
Lists recruitment consultants specialising in voluntary sector
appointments.
<www.volresource.org.uk/workopps/recruit.htm>

## Wales Council for Voluntary Action (WCVA)

# Index